Financial Tactics and Terms for the Sophisticated International Investor

Also by Harry D. Schultz

Bear Markets—How to Survive and Make Money in Them

The Dollar Devaluation—Mechanics and Timing

Handbook for Using and Understanding Swiss Banks

How to Keep Your Money and Freedom

Inflation and Financial Hedges

The International Monetary Muddle

Panics and Crashes and How You Can Make Money Out of Them

A Treasury of Wall Street Wisdom

What the Prudent Investor Should Know About Switzerland—
and Foreign Money Havens

Harry D. Schultz

Financial Tactics and Terms for the Sophisticated International Investor

Harper & Row, Publishers

New York
Evanston
San Francisco
London

Library of Congress Cataloging in Publication Data

Schultz, Harry D
  Financial tactics and terms for the sophisticated international investor.

  1. Investments—Dictionaries.   2. International finance—Dictionaries.
I. Title.
HG4513.S33   332.6′03   72-9152
ISBN 0-06-013808-4

FIRST EDITION

Designed by Dorothy Schmiderer

To my staff—
English, Canadian, American, and Swiss—
who helped so much
in putting this volume together

Introduction

Books should not be written unless they fill a genuine need.

And thus *this* book.

It provides several things that were missing in the realms of money investing. There have been an incredible number of *changes* in the investment world in recent years. Very few people (if any) have managed to understand all the wrinkles, all the terms, all the techniques that have grown around these changes, things like Eurodollars, what are they and how you use them.

Americans have discovered their dollar isn't what it used to be. Many found they lose money through devaluation and hear about other dollar devaluations coming. What to do about it?

And Americans found their stock market wasn't as profitable as it had been. Many investors lost money in 1972. They heard that stock markets in other countries did much better. Some found ways to cash in on it. But this requires expanding the mind to take in new strategies and make new habits.

It's also a book for those who don't believe free enterprise is dead.

And it's a book of secrets and revelations about the world of money placement.

There's plenty of savvy behind it. Virtually every word herein is gleaned from personal experience, of my own and/or staff members. There are no ivory towers in this book.

Capital preservation began taking on a new meaning in 1972, as inflation raged and the stock market was off and taxes rose. *Buying power* took on new meaning. So new attitudes about preserving capital began to emerge. It meant people who never tried their hand in certain areas of money placement had to learn new terminology and technique.

And then, too, there never has been a proper reference book for the whole area of money.

So for all these and a few more reasons too, this book was seen by my publishers as a real need. I was glad to write it because it will save my having to answer so many letters I get from readers of my investment newsletter, asking for explanations of new-era money management. They aren't letters from beginners, either. Even those who make investing a full-time job aren't usually conversant with every aspect of financing: bonds, Eurocurrencies, foreign stock markets, commodity trading, new issues, and so on. Nobody is a walking dictionary of money. But now, with this book, you can be one (more or less).

Some will use it as a reference book. But I hope you'll read it like a sexy novel. It has no story line, but there *is* a theme. That theme is: you can increase your buying power through knowledge.

Harry D. Schultz

Basel, Switzerland

Acceptance

An accepted time draft or bill of exchange. The term is also used for the act of taking in these drafts and bills of payment, according to pre-arranged terms. (See also **Bank Acceptance.**)

Acceptance Houses

Banks in England whose chief activity used to be in the field of discounting acceptances. (See **Bank Acceptance.**) Over a period of time such acceptance houses have developed all the other types of banking functions but have retained a privileged status in the British banking community because of their former key position in the country's monetary and banking system.

Account Executive

One refers to an account executive usually in the context of either the brokerage business (i.e., stock-market brokerage) or the advertising business. An account executive is a person who deals directly with clients, generating and running their accounts. (See **Brokers.**)

Accrual and Accrue

In the financial world one speaks of accrual when income or expenses are building up but are not actually being taken in or paid out. For example, a company may have bank debts or bonds outstanding upon which it must periodically pay interest. Normally a corporation will steadily accrue the interest obligations without immediately paying them since outpayments are foreseen at specific times, often once a year. This means that a corporation may, every month, set aside 1/12th of the amount due at the end of the one-year period. These accruals would build up so that in the final month, before the actual payment had to be made, 11/12ths of the amount would have been accumulated on an accrual basis.

Actuary

A person who develops insurance tables. On the basis of statistics and applying mathematical principles, he evaluates such risks as that of a person's dying at a certain age or becoming ill x number of times during a given period. From these calculations he determines what the premium must be on a given type of insurance. Actuarial tables are the data laid out by actuaries.

Advance-Decline Line

A running cumulative numerical total plotted as a line on a chart. It is obtained by subtracting the daily declines from advances (or vice versa) and then adding or subtracting the difference from a running total,

ADVANCE-DECLINE LINE

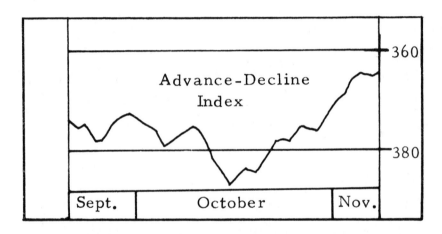

starting with an arbitrary figure. The resulting index shows what the great mass of the market is doing, for it embraces the trend of the entire market, in contrast to the limited number of stocks embodied in the Dow-Jones Industrial Average or any other stock average used in market analysis. Its significance is especially noteworthy when it *diverges* from the stock averages. For example, the Dow might be climbing while the advance-decline line is falling, showing that while a few stocks may be "leading the market" the majority of the market isn't following in any real sense. This would make the DJIA more suspect and a reversal could be at hand. Conversely, it would be bullish if the advance-decline line rose faster than the stock averages.

Advice Note

A note sent by a bank or a brokerage company to a customer giving him the details of a financial transaction carried out on his behalf. For example, one can receive an advice note saying that the broker has brought 100 ATT at a price of $200, resulting in a debit charge to the client of $20,000 (plus the broker's charges). An advice note from a bank can inform the customer that the bank has placed $50,000 dollars in the Eurodollar market for 6 months at the rate of 6 percent per annum and that the bank's fee for such a placement will involve ½ of 1 percent per annum.

Advisory Services

Investment letters, or advisory services, on stock-market or commodity-market analysis fall into a number of categories. There are those put out by brokerage houses, which generally tend to be worth what they cost; they are sent to customers, usually free of charge. Among analysts who charge for their services the prices vary widely, as do the methods used to attempt to determine the future direction of various markets. Some use pure technical analysis (see **Analyst** and **Technical Analysis**), and this method is quite useful, especially when only domestic economic and financial elements are involved. But in recent years, with the international monetary and political scene playing a more and more important part in the function and circulation of money and thus indirectly in the movement of capital in and out of stocks, technical analysis has been most useful in the context of the bigger picture. Other services use fundamental facts to base their recommendations, and a few use both methods. There is no way of judging the usefulness of an advisory service except by observing it over a period of time and assessing its accuracy rate of prognostication. In the United States, subscription prices are mainly in the range of $100 to $200 a year, though some are $50 to $75 and a few about $500. Foreign advisory letters are much cheaper, ranging from $20 to $100 in the main.

Advisory services worth investigating. Indicator Digest: An indicator research probably second to none in comprehensiveness. Very much a technical service. Published in Palisades Park, N. J., 07650. *Dow Theory Letters*: Issued by Richard Russell (P.O. Box 1759, La Jolla, Cal.

92037). He does not confine himself to the Dow Theory, but he does tend to specialize in technical factors on the market. *The Dines Letter*: A point and figure chart and advisory service published at 18 East 41st Street, New York, N.Y. 10017. *Bank Credit Analyst*: An excellent service specializing in banking and credit indicators. Published at 1245 Sherbrooke Street West, Montreal, Quebec. *Drew Odd Lot Studies*: The dean of odd-lot indicators is Garfield Drew. His service emphasizes these statistics but not to the exclusion of all else. Published at 50 Congress Street, Boston, Mass. 02109. *Bank Index Theory*: This service has a unique concept of forecasting based on an original index of Canadian banking shares. Published by H. E. Boulter, 25 Adelaide Street E. W., Toronto 1, Ontario. *International Harry Schultz Letter*: My own publication, which covers the international aspects of politico-economics and how it affects your investments at home and abroad, plus foreign exchange, gold, and currency trading. It forecasts all world stock markets. Published at Box 1161, Basel, 4002, Switzerland. (Or you can write to Suite 226, 67 Yonge Street, Toronto 1, Ontario.)

There is not enough room here to mention all the investment services, and mentioning a few is no slur on those unlisted. You might, for example, like to investigate John Kamin's Forecaster, Myers' Financial Review, Cumulative Average, Alden Wells, Holt Advisory, George Schaeffer, Frank Buck, Baxter's Report, George Lindsay, Banson Reports, Edson Gould, Lawry's Reports, Trendex, Tillman Survey, Don Worden, Chartcraft, Joe Granville, Bob Geisinger, Lynch International Investment Survey, John Magee, Paul Dysart, Martin Zweig, Space Time Forecasting, and especially the American Institute for Economic Research—one of the oldest and best in its particular field. There are many others, but most not mentioned here are less than three years old.

Affluent

A term that has gained common usage largely as a result of the publication of J. K. Galbraith's *The Affluent Society*. It is employed to describe a person or group of people or society that has reached a high standard of living. It is used specifically these days as almost synonymous with the consumer society, often in a more or less derogatory sense to describe a society which has so much that it is caught up in the momentum of replacing unnecessary items as fast as the advertising men can persuade it to do so. It is frequently used in speaking of a prosperous but sick society, and/or one that is not content with its great wealth.

After Market

Secondary market for any kind of financial paper. After a new bond issue, for example, has been initially sold, subsequent buying and selling must be done in the after market, which is made by bond dealers and banks. Certificates of deposit can be sold in their own after market.

Agio

An Italian word meaning "premium." An agio is the premium paid for a security or a currency over its par value. Usually agio, which is commonly employed throughout continental Europe, is expressed in terms of percentage of par value. For example, if a security has a par value of $100 and is selling for $110, the agio is 10 percent.

Alchemy

A pseudoscience that can be traced back as far as the early Egyptians and that reached its greatest prominence around the sixteenth century. Alchemists believe that it is possible chemically to turn base metals (copper and lead) into gold and silver. The original premise was based on a theory of the ancients that the universe was made of some sort of basic substance and that all things in it were merely stages of progression of that substance. Hence it followed that one could merely move along the progression to change a base metal into a precious metal. In a sense, this theory has had scientific proof in the modern discovery of the atom. Alchemy also had been used loosely in the twentieth century in an economic sense in reference to those government officials who try to pretend that paper money is as good as gold and who in fact are attempting to practice a modern form of alchemy in attempting to convince the public that anything can have the properties of precious metals if you *say* so loud and long enough.

American Depository Receipts (ADRs)

Instruments issued by American banks as counterparts for foreign securities. If you are an American citizen and decide to invest in the shares of a South African gold mine or of a German industrial company, you would normally buy and sell American depository receipts. The system works as follows: first the bank involved buys the security in the foreign market and deposits the security in its name at a correspondent bank abroad. It then issues an American depository receipt (ADR), which gives its owner ultimate claim on the security. ADRs make the physical handling of securities much easier, precluding the need for constant physical shipment back and forth between countries, which involves not only expense but often a great deal of time and frustration. However, the actual mechanics of the ADR system, like the actual mechanics of the short sale, are of no real concern to the average investor. Once an ADR on a foreign stock has been acquired in the United States, that ADR is bought and sold through brokerage houses like any normal share. The main difference between the ADR and the actual share on the foreign market is that the ADR will sell for about 10 percent more, owing to the fact that the first time the share was brought into the United States, the interest-equalization tax was paid on it, and thereafter that tax became part of its actual price for all future purchases and sales to other Americans. If you own an ADR, however, and wish for some reason to revert it to a foreign share traded abroad, then the whole process of putting it through a bank has to be performed in reverse.

American Stock Exchange

The smaller of the great New York securities markets. It originated at the time of the great California gold rush in 1849, when shares of the new gold-mining corporations were introduced on this Curb Exchange, so called because its dealings actually occurred on Broad Street in the open air, "on the curb." In 1921 the exchange moved into its own building. Traditionally, the smaller companies and corporations and new companies have been listed on the American Stock Exchange. In the past it has been usual that once a corporation reached a certain size and had gained major recognition by the U.S. financial community, it would transfer its listing to the **New York Stock Exchange** (see). However, in recent years the American Stock Exchange has greatly tightened its requirements for listings and is today in almost every respect comparable to the Big Board except in size. The American Stock Exchange represents (as a whole) a more speculative aspect of Wall Street than does the New York Stock Exchange; hence it is worth watching, since blue chips alone never made a bull or bear market. The New York Stock Exchange cannot create and maintain a bull or bear movement by itself, and therefore a disparity between the two markets is a factor to watch for. When the New York Stock Exchange is moving up quite strongly, for example, but the American is standing still or moving down, then the movement on the Big Board is suspect. The American Stock Exchange, housing smaller companies and those which are more sensitive to prime movements than those on the senior exchange, tends to show the "breadth" of a market move. If the two markets are moving in divergence, it tends to mean that what is happening to, say, the Dow-Jones Average is limited to a relatively few stocks. A merger of the two exchanges is being considered. ASE is the symbol commonly used to designate the junior exchange.

Amortization

Accountancy term employed for the write-down, or reduction in value, of assets. This is often found on the balance sheet of a corporation. To demonstrate how amortization works, let us take as an example a TV-set producer. Some manufacturers have to maintain inventories of various types of components, for example video tubes. Such inventories are normally listed as assets on the balance sheets of these companies in terms of what the company paid for them. A number of years ago the entire industry shifted from tubes to transistors for many of the functions inside a TV set. As a result, the tubes listed in such companies' inventories assets suddenly lost some or all of their value. This required their amortization, or the write-down of these assets. *All* equipment is amortized, usually in accordance with fixed standards or tables. A typewriter can be written off in *x* years as well as a press or stamping machine. The purpose is to provide funds to buy new equipment as replacements.

Amsterdam

Largest city of the Netherlands. Its history as a financial capital goes
back several centuries. The reason for the early employment of Amsterdam as a European financial center was that the Netherlands, like
England, acquired a large overseas empire, and a vast amount of trade
developed between the mother country and her overseas territories. Because of the constant movement of goods going out in the form of Dutch
manufactures to such overseas territories, and coming in as raw materials from such areas as the Dutch East Indies (Indonesia) or the
West Indies, a large amount of interim financing was necessary (that
is, financing of the period when such goods were in transit). This resulted in the development of an acceptance market in Amsterdam
parallel to that in London. (See **Bank Acceptance** and **Acceptance
Houses**.) It further resulted in the establishment of an exchange in
Amsterdam dealing in short-term monetary instruments and foreign exchange and finally in stocks and securities. The East India Company
of Amsterdam was one of the world's first corporations with issued share
capital. Already in the seventeenth century more than a hundred different types of securities were being traded on the Amsterdam market by
various foreign powers. In the second half of the nineteenth century
Amsterdam played a very important role in financing the development
and construction of railroads in the United States and also in providing
capital to American industries and distribution organizations. Amsterdam
had a major setback during both the First and Second World Wars, when
the international activities of the city as a financial center ceased. Following World War II the Dutch adopted a very open policy, and the
Amsterdam exchange was one of the first to court a listing of non-Dutch
securities, especially those from the United States. Amsterdam now
ranks with Frankfurt and Zurich as one of the most important financial
centers in Germanic-speaking Europe.

Analyst

In the securities industry, a person who devotes himself to the study
of securities and/or securities markets. Usually the analyst specializes in
one or two industries. For instance, there are analysts who devote themselves to the steel industry, others to the oil industry, and still others

to the electronics industry. Their method of approach varies, but generally they rely heavily upon the published financial material relating to a company as well as on conversations with executives, scientists, and engineers of the corporation (or industry) involved. On the basis of these facts, conversations, and statistics, they form a conclusion about the future of the company, especially its future earnings, and make a judgment as to whether a security should be bought or, if already owned, sold or held. Some analysts also employ chart analysis (See **Charts and Chart Reading**), in which case they do not depend primarily on fundamentals (i.e., specific corporate facts and figures) but rather on the *performance* of the stock or bond or warrant in the securities markets as such. These chartists keep a record of price movements and the volume of trading of a stock, then chart this on different types of graph paper and form their conclusions as to future price movements from the patterns of such price action.

There is only one way to judge the abilities of an analyst, and that is by his past performance. This of course assumes that one is using an analyst for his ability to interpret statistics and not just for his ability to gather a certain type of statistical data together. To use the analyst most effectively once you have chosen him, you *must* trust him. If you listen to an analyst's advice and then try to outguess him, the chances are you will double the error and never double the chances of being right. Also, if you take an analyst's advice to get into an investment situation, then you must use the same analyst to get out of it. Money is not made by buying stocks; it is made by selling them, and whoever tells you to get into a stock has good reasons, and so on the basis of those same lines of reasoning will have the best knowledge of when to advise you to get out of them.

Andorra

One of the newest tax havens for victimized millionaires. The only significant tax in Andorra is a 2 percent import duty. There are no death duties, no income tax, no customs formalities on either entering or leaving (Andorra customs, that is), no purchase tax, no corporation tax (although only one third foreign capital is allowed on companies promoted in Andorra). Andorra is a country of about 190 square miles in the Pyrenees Mountains between France and Spain. It is run by a local council of 24 and a police force of 20. There are about 20,000 inhabitants. Residency is easy; but if you are thinking of setting up nonresident corporations (corporations registered there but doing no business there), and indeed if you decide to live there, the problem is transport. The nearest airport is at Barcelona, 151 miles away. The mountain roads are kept open all year, but even in the best weather traveling to and fro is hardly a joyride. A place to retire, maybe, but not so much for people on the go.

Annual Report

The compulsory yearly accounting made by a **public corporation** (see). The purpose of such annual reports is to keep shareholders informed about the status and progress of "their" corporation. One must not only read the main group of numbers but should also carefully scrutinize the footnotes attached to these financial statements. Often such footnotes will run to forty or fifty items, and often it is here that problems or other financial aspects of the corporation that have not been mentioned anywhere else in the report come to light, thanks to the legal requirements that such things be mentioned by the accountants in their statements before they can be certified. Watch for such items as the possible dilution that may affect you as a shareholder as a result of the potential for the conversion of debentures into common shares. Other things to watch for are the possibilities for executives of the corporation to exercise options on shares of your company—also a potential for substantial dilution. Finally, now and then footnotes are added in regard to debts owed to banks where special conditions are attached; these may indicate that the corporation has liquidity problems that do not come out in the body of the report.

Annuity

Term usually employed for insurance policies that provide the policyholder with an annual payment after he reaches a certain age. It must be remembered that an annuity is not an insurance policy in the usual sense, but that its prime purpose is to provide a pension (or annual payment) starting at some future date. In times of increasing global inflation, annuities are one of the most badly hit forms of investment. A hard-working man can pay into this type of insurance for years, only to discover when it comes time to draw on it that inflation has taken away much or most of the value the payments would have had in terms of buying power. If you are considering buying annuities during these inflationary times, you would be well advised to look for any that have a provision that makes them increase in ratio to the cost of living, or some other inflation-observation index.

Anstalten. See **Liechtenstein**

Antitrust Laws

Introduced in the United States in the form of the Sherman Anti-Trust Act of 1890. They were aimed at blocking business trusts and/or cartels. These cartels and trusts are groupings of companies, usually in the same field, designed to eliminate competition where their particular range of products is concerned. The rationale of these laws is that the entire nation and especially the consumer are hurt when such trusts and cartels are formed, since the laws of supply and demand (as they especially relate to pricing) are disrupted and artificial prices and artificial profits can be derived by small groups of companies from their interruption of the normal competitive process. The antitrust philosophy has also been adopted by the European Common Market and will probably be progressively applied there in the decade to come, though undoubtedly much less stringently than in the United States.

Arbitrage

Simultaneous buying and selling of a security, currency, commodity, etc., when it is traded on different markets at slightly different prices. The object is to make a profit on the difference in the price. For example, ADR shares (see **American Depository Receipts**) sell (or should sell) at exactly the interest-equalization tax differential from the price of the share in its country of origin. If this gets out of line and, say, the ADR is selling for a higher premium than the exact amount of the tax, then you could in theory buy the stock in South Africa, for example, and get an ADR put on it and sell it in New York at the same time, making a neat instant profit. However, arbitrage is a highly sophisticated form of trading and should not be attempted by the novice. A man who understands arbitrage can exploit the price difference between any two markets, allowing him to buy something where it is cheaper and sell it in another market at exactly the same time where it is more expensive. Such arbitrage is practiced principally in the field of foreign exchange, securities, interest, money markets, and commodities. An example: Dow Chemical is traded on both the New York and Zurich exchanges (as are many U.S. shares). At times there will be a differential in their prices on which a small arbitrage can be made.

Arithmetical Graph Paper

In the field of technical analysis and stock charting there are two distinct schools of thought on how charts of stocks should be made. One school believes that when prices of stocks go up or down, what is important is the dollar or *money* increase or decrease. This school uses graph paper with equal-size squares for their charts, thus giving equal value to every dollar movement, whether the stock is $2 a share or $300 a share. The other school believes that the *percentage* increase or

EXAMPLES OF ARITHMETICAL AND SEMILOGARITHMIC CHART PAPER

Semilogarithmic Chart Paper obtainable from John Magee, 360 Worthington Street, Springfield 3, Mass.

decrease in a stock is what matters, and they chart on what is known as semilogarithmic paper (unequal-size squares), which shows percentage increase or decrease. For example, a stock selling at $2 moving to $4 would show the same degree of movement as a stock of $100 moving to $200, since each is a 100 percent move. The answer of who is right

ARITHMETICAL CHART PAPER

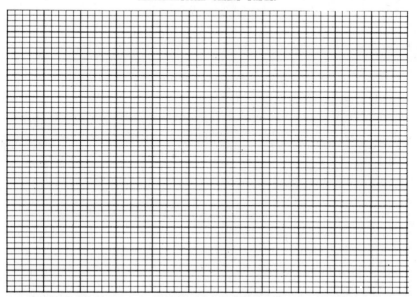

has never been solved, but from my own experience I would say that percentage movement has its greatest validity on a very long-term basis (multiyear charts) and that the small day-to-day movements are more valid for forecasting when expressed in pure money terms on arithmetical graph paper.

Asset

Accountancy term for something of value owned by a person, association, or corporation. Normally in business such assets are in the form of land, plant and equipment inventories, prepaid expenses, cash, accounts receivable, etc. Exceptionally, corporations also list such items as research and development or goodwill as an asset, since if the ownership of such intangibles were transferred to another person he would be expected to pay a price for them.

Assignment

Endorsement of an asset to another party. This procedure is especially used when transferring securities, property, etc., in trust or for the benefit of creditors.

Assignats

Currency issued by the French Revolutionary government between 1790 and 1795, consisting of notes based on productive real estate. The hyperinflation that resulted because of this land-backed currency is the biggest economic disaster in French history. At the end of the fiasco, currency was actually *annulled* rather than being merely devalued. For further information on this period I recommend *Fiat Money Inflation in France,* by Andrew Dickson White, 1959 (Caxton Printers, Ltd., 312 Main Street, Caldwell, Idaho 83605).

Assurance

A word widely used in the United Kingdom and Europe, everywhere in fact except in the United States, for insurance.

At-the-Market Orders

When placing an order to buy or sell stock in the market, one can use any number of methods. You can determine the point at which a stock becomes a sale or a buy for you and place the specific price as an order with your broker. Or you can decide that now is the time you want action and place an "at-the-market" order. This means that your broker or banker will telephone your order through, and whatever price is being quoted on the floor of the exchange when your order gets there is the price you will actually get. (See also **Buy Orders and Sell Orders**.)

Audit

Examination of the status of a person, association, or corporation, especially the *financial* status as determined by accountants or auditors. The primary function of an audit is to verify that all assets and liabilities, income and expenses, are correctly reflected in the books of a corporation. Normally at the end of an audit the auditor will verify publicly that the published annual (or quarterly) statement and attached financial statement are correct. One can also use the term "audit" in regard to other types of surveys. For instance, a management audit would involve the examination of the capabilities of a management group or team as to their effectiveness. A tax audit seeks to verify the veracity of income and expense previously reported.

Australia

Financially, still the land of opportunity. It is also a land of sunshine and sportsmen, and the main social life in the country takes place in the great out-of-doors, as in swimming and fishing. For all the vastness of Australia, only the fringes are habitable. Americans generally get along very well in Australia, for the Australians are probably nearer to Americans in temperament than are any other people in the world. Australians are friendly and hospitable, and the country is so much safer than the United States that many Americans have made their home there. For investment purposes the main interest in Australia is its mining wealth; every month there seems to be new finds of minerals of one sort or another. Immigration to Australia is easy, particularly for North Americans, but before you can apply for citizenship you must have lived there for five years. Taxation is unfortunately quite heavy in Australia, being progressive up to about 67 percent on incomes over 20,000 Australian dollars. A tax on dividends and interest payable to nonresidents is levied at the rate of 30 percent, deducted at source. Australia has exchange control, foolishly copied from the English. Company taxation runs from 32.5 percent to 47.5 percent, depending on the type of company and the amount of profit.

Austria

Little known is the fact that Austria offers the most secret of all bank accounts, though its use is so restricted as to be of limited use to foreigners. I refer to the personal passbook account. Everyone in Austria seems to have one. It goes only by a number and is open theoretically only to Austrians. Actually, no questions are asked if you open such an account. But it must be opened in person, and if you don't speak German some banks might refuse you. The government can't pry into it because the bank doesn't even have your name and address. The passbook is the only record, and the bank knows you only by number.

Austria, just next door to Switzerland and a Germanic country, has a lot of differences from its neighbors. Austria was once the hub of one of the greatest empires in Europe, and the country still bears an imperial atmosphere. It is the most cultured and refined of the German countries and is a very happy place. Its closeness to the Iron Curtain and Eastern Europe (day trips run from Vienna to Hungary and Czechoslovakia) does give some visitors a slightly uncomfortable feeling, but if it bothers the Austrians they don't show it. The climate is temperate and of its 7.5 million population one million live in Vienna. Austria is a federal republic with a parliament. . . . *Income tax:* This is paid by Austrian nationals and residents of Austria on worldwide income on a progressive sliding scale. For example, on an income of about $5,000 one would pay about 33 percent. *Corporation tax:* up to $40,000 per year, 24 percent; over that, 44 percent. *Property tax:* 0.75 percent per annum. *Capital gains:* 15 percent. Austria is certainly not a tax haven, and indeed is only to be considered as a place to live should you just want a civilized Germanic atmosphere. Residency can be obtained provided you go through the necessary channels, but citizenship can be granted only aften ten years of domicile in Austria. Investment in Austrian shares has been profitable in the 1970s, though foreign participation is minimal. The Austrian schilling is considered a relatively strong currency.

Autarky

A national policy under which a nation seeks to achieve self-sufficiency by seeking to reduce its dependency on any other nation for its supplies of raw materials, manufactured goods, or even services by replacing them with national production. Usually, strong nationalism or a strong nationalistic policy goes hand in hand with autarky.

Avoidance and Evasion

These two words have special senses in connection with taxation. Tax avoidance is permitted, tax evasion is not. Evasion is a criminal offense in the United States and can result in a jail sentence. Tax avoidance occurs when, with the help of a good tax lawyer, you set up your taxable assets in such a way as to take full advantage of the law. It is probably true that most people who do not consult a tax lawyer and who have income from sources other than a straight salary pay more tax than they need to. The IRS is not going to point out to a private individual that if he set up a company instead of being self-employed, or if he used a trust or whatever, he could pay less in taxes. It is up to the individual to find this out for himself, through tax avoidance. Tax evasion, in contrast, is deliberate lawbreaking. It is hiding money in bank accounts abroad with the intention of not paying tax on the interest or capital gains when invested. It is taking payment in cash and keeping no record of such payments being made and so no tax being levied. It is blowing up expenses beyond what can be substantiated in order to claim more against taxes; it is keeping two sets of books, one for the government and one for real; etc., etc. Many contend that fiscal violations are not dangerous and do not cause violence to citizens, and thus do not deserve to be called criminal offenses. Many nations share this view. Some people feel that making tax evasion criminal is justice falling back to the level of the Bastille, when people were imprisoned for stealing food. Debtors' prisons and jails for tax evaders have ominous similarities that upset many to whom justice is the prime criterion for judging human progress.

Bahamas

A tax haven. The Bahamas are a chain of islands starting less than 75 miles east of Florida. There are about 700 islands in the Bahamas group but only 30 are inhabited. The Bahamas are a very expensive place to live, for virtually everything is imported. The Bahamas (the town of Nassau in particular) sell tax-haven status the way many countries sell postage stamps. They literally sell a brass plate for a lawyer's front door. More than 12,000 companies are registered in the Bahamas, most of which do no business on the islands at all. Bahamas taxation, or the lack of it, is of course the main attraction. There is no income tax, no corporation tax, no capital-gains tax, no withholding tax, no estate duty. A tax on share capital of 0.058 percent and on loan capital of 0.115 percent is levied once, either when the company is authorized or when it increases its capital. A stamp tax of 0.25 percent is levied on all money remitted abroad (new regulations may alter currency export now; consult a U.S., Canadian, or British bank there). A real-property tax, based on market value, is levied at the rate of 0.5 percent on all developed property on the island of New Providence (on which stands Nassau).

Grand Bahama-Freeport Area: a tax-free zone where licensees of the Grand Bahama Port Authority, Ltd., have been given a "tax holiday" until 1990. There is total tax exemption until 1990 to manufacturing companies starting operations on a commercial scale anywhere in Bahamas before December 31, 1975.

Residency and Citizenship: A visitor may stay in the Bahamas for a maximum of eight months. For a longer stay one must apply to the Director of Immigration, P.O. Box 831, Nassau, for an annual residency permit. This does not entitle the holder to work. There is technically no such thing as a Bahamian citizen—the Bahamas are a self-governing British colony, hence local Bahamians are British subjects with Bahamian status. To acquire such a status has required a minimum of five years' residency. However, the Bahamas have voted for separation from Britain. With the gradual coming of independence for the Bahamas have come some quite unfriendly banking laws. Work permits become increasingly difficult to obtain, and the whole atmosphere of the islands is becoming unconducive to tax-haven business. Hence the current trend of many people who have been operating there is to move from the Bahamas to the **Cayman Islands** (see), which, as a new tax haven, exert themselves to be nice to the victimized millionaire and encourage his business.

Balance of Payments

A summary of the international transactions of a country or region over a fixed period of time, including commodity and service transactions, capital transactions, and gold movements. It is the difference (on the plus or minus side) between total payments taken in from abroad and payments made to other countries. The payments may be made in the form of foreign currencies or gold. In short, it is the result of international trading. A country with a balance-of-payments deficit has imported more goods and services than it has sold abroad, and one with a surplus has sold more goods abroad than it has imported. The imbalance can be caused because of differences in productivity in the home country relative to those abroad (e.g., perhaps a neighboring country can produce more goods per man-hour than your own country can and thus sell them cheaper), or it can be simply that the domestic currency of a particular country is over- or underpriced, relative to other countries. These days it is fashionable (in Washington at least) to blame all balance-of-payments imbalances on currency malvalues, and never to give any credit to a country that simply produces more, faster, better, and of better quality than others can. If a nation succeeds in business these days (e.g., Japan) that nation is *told* to reduce its surplus. This sour-apples attitude is an about-face for the United States, which formerly believed the supreme merit was to work hard and be competitive and show a profit.

It should also be mentioned here that balance-of-payments inflow and outflows are caused by another factor than those of trade listed above— to wit, capital movement. This occurs when businessmen and investors move their money out of one country (perhaps because they have fears about its currency stability) and into another (where they feel the currency or economy is stronger). This has recently become a major factor in BOP surplus and deficit totals. It is sometimes called "hot money" because of its quick movement. But many very conservative investors move money slowly and with deliberation as their faith in a country (politically, socially, for currency, or for business) ebbs. This is in effect voting with one's feet, although the term has more meaning under a gold standard. Even so, it represents money going out because of diminishing confidence in the management of any given country.

Balance Sheet

A listing of the assets and liabilities of a corporation. By definition, according to accountancy practices, the asset and liability columns must always be in balance (i.e., have identical totals). A balance sheet gives a summary of the financial condition of any company. Normally it is issued once a year and published in the annual report.

Bands, Currency. See Currency Bands

Bank Acceptance

An acceptance is an accepted draft or bill of exchange, and a bank acceptance is one that has been signed by a bank. In contrast to a trade acceptance, it is not related to any goods but rather is a financial bill of exchange backed by the assets of the bank itself.

Bankers' Almanac

A massive handbook or reference book which has been published annually in London since 1834. It lists the most important banks in the entire world and also contains the key financial data on each of them, as well as the names of its key officers. The publisher is Thomas Skinner & Co., Ltd., 30 Finsbury Square, London, E.C. 2, England.

Bank for International Settlements

An institution whose purpose is to further cooperation between the central banks of the world, to create new opportunities for development of financial transactions on an intergovernmental basis, and to act as a trustee or agent in regard to international contracts or agreements involving the transfer of payments. The BIS, founded in 1930 on the basis of a 1929 conference on war reparations at The Hague, is situated in Basel, Switzerland. Its capital is 500 million Swiss gold francs, of which one quarter is paid in. Ownership of the bank is divided among 200,000 registered shares, of which approximately three quarters belong to European central banks and one quarter to private persons. The shares of the bank may be transferred to other owners only with the agreement of both the bank itself and the central banks that hold the majority interest.

The bank has supranational immunity. It is not subject to any Swiss taxes or to any laws that might be applied in Switzerland regarding the restrictions on the import and export of gold or foreign exchange, nor is it subject to expropriation or any such measures. At the beginning of its existence its prime function was to serve as an agent in regard to the issue and management of the loans involved under the 1929 Young Plan for the collection of war reparations. Later it served as an agent for loans issued by the high authority of the European Coal and Steel Community in Luxembourg. Its primary function today is that of a clearinghouse or for exchanges of opinions among the leading central banks of the world. The heads of the central banks of the United States, Great Britain, Japan, West Germany, France, Belgium, the Netherlands, Italy, Sweden, and Switzerland meet each month in Basel, always over a weekend and usually on Sunday morning and again Sunday afternoon. It is there that strategic decisions regarding international monetary problems are often made.

Bank Holiday

Holiday on which the banks do not open. The term is used especially in the United Kingdom. It takes on a special meaning in times of war or economic crisis, when bank holidays are declared by governments to preclude runs on the banks. This occurred in many countries in the early 1930s.

Bank Index Theory. See Advisory Services

Banking

For practically as far back as written history goes, we have records of banking in some form or other, although its form has changed radically over the years. There are records of banking loans and exchanges as far back as 6000 B.C. Early banking "institutions" were often little more than moneychangers in the temples and sacred places. Probably one reason they operated there was a belief that as such places were protected by the gods they would be less likely to be robbed, and thus were ideal for setting up a business whose main commodity was money. By the fourth century B.C. in Greece, public bodies and private firms were accepting deposits, making loans, changing coins, and dealing with the mechanics of international trade (i.e., the movement of specie between international cities). With the fall of the Roman Empire there was a vast decline in international trade, so there was little use for extensive banking facilities. Banking as we know it didn't emerge until the rebirth of international trade around the thirteenth and fourteenth centuries, and seems to have originated generally in Italy. Hence commercial banking in the sense we know it today really only evolved in the later Middle Ages, from the much older institutions of moneylending and moneychanging. Right down to fairly recent times, the concept that government should be solely responsible for issuance of coin and paper and should make laws about currency was not generally accepted. Banknotes and coin, like other commodities, were usually regarded as the prerogative of private enterprise; and it was incumbent on the issuer to stand behind his obligation with something of value, freely convertible into it.

Bank, Merchant. See **Merchant Bank**

Bank Notes

Nowadays usually nothing more than paper money issued by the governments of most countries, which also guarantee their value and validity. Thus they are really governmental notes, not bank notes. The first bank notes of modern times were issued by the Bank of England in 1694, although archeological findings have proved that bank notes were known in China before the Christian era. Originally they had the function of deposit certificates. That is, they were certificates or notes issued against the deposit of a certain sum of valuable coins. In other words, the original bank notes were backed up by coins that had a definite intrinsic value, and in effect the notes were warehouse receipts. At first governments that issued bank notes usually felt obligated to issue such notes only in amounts covered by their holdings of gold and silver bullion. But today the bank notes of most countries are no longer backed by anything of specific value such as precious metals. They are backed by nothing else than faith in the ability of the issuing government to protect their value. Bank notes, and especially their constant issue, have been one of the prime reasons for the secular inflation of the twentieth century. It may well be that in a few decades the use of bank notes will diminish substantially as their function is taken over by credit cards, Giro (see **Postal Checking Systems**), and other types of systems under which payments can be made without the actual physical use of bank notes or the like.

Bank of England

Central bank of the United Kingdom. In 1694 the English state, in return for a loan of 1.2 million pounds sterling from a privately owned corporation, gave that corporation the right to carry on bank business under the name of the Governor and Company of the Bank of England. The current organization of the Bank of England is based mainly on the Bank Act of 1844, during the Peel ministry, in which the issuance of bank notes was separated from other types of banking activities. It was transferred to the issue department of the bank, whereas other activities were retained in what has become known as the banking department. The two departments publish separate statements. Through the Bank of England Act of 1946, the capital of the bank was transferred from private hands into public hands. Yet the Bank of England still continues as a separate legal entity, not a part of the government, even though, according to the law of 1946, the Chancellor of the Exchequer is authorized to give instructions to the bank or to the governors of the Bank of England. The Bank Act of 1844 governing the activities of the Bank of England was based on the principle that notes to be issued and in circulation had to be completely covered by gold. But as early as the First World War, currency notes were being issued without gold cover, and they were finally legalized as a permanent form of currency by the Currency and Bank Notes Act of 1928. This act allowed the Bank of England to increase money in circulation without any gold cover, provided it had the permission of the Treasury, although no parliamentary control was established. By the Currency and Bank Notes Act of February 28, 1939, all pretense of gold cover was abandoned and the gold stocks of the Bank of England were transferred to the Exchequer.

Bank Rate

Key interest rate in the banking system; the rate at which the central bank of a country lends to its own money-market institutions. The movement of this rate will, in general, have an effect on all interest rates. For example, if the central bank raises the bank rate, then short-term interest rates that commercial banks pay on deposits will rise, along with interest on such things as Treasury bills. This prime-rate manipulation enables the government of a country, through its central bank, to exert pressure on the banking institutions of that country to help it "tighten" or "free" the money flow.

Bankruptcy

The status, declared by law, of a debtor unable to pay his debts. It means that the debtor does not have in any form (i.e., property, securities, receivables, cash, etc.) sufficient means to meet his outstanding debts. If he does have the means but his assets are tied up in property or other nonliquid assets, then he is merely said to be insolvent. When bankruptcy is declared to be the debtor's status and some form of settlement has been worked out by the bankruptcy court (for example, if a man has some assets but not enough to meet all his obligations, then he might be required by the court to pay, say, ten cents of every dollar owed to his creditors), the debtor is legally discharged from any further obligation for these debts. A petition of bankruptcy may be filed by creditors in an attempt to recover at least part of what is owed them, or it may be brought by the debtor, who finds himself getting into deeper and deeper water financially and uses this way to clear the slate and start again.

Bank Secrecy

Usually identified with Switzerland. There, since the 1930s, any bank officer or employee revealing any secrets of a bank to an outside party is subject to criminal penalties. This provision is anchored in Article 47 of the Swiss Bank Law. The penalties involved are fines up to 20,000 Swiss francs or prison up to six months, or both if it is a serious case. The law is primarily aimed at preventing an employee of any Swiss bank from revealing the names of bank clients to an outside person or authority or from revealing the nature of any transactions made by the bank for its clients or for itself. The philosophy of bank secrecy goes well back into the nineteenth century, when it was recognized as accepted practice on the same level as that which requires medical doctors or lawyers to maintain the confidentiality of their relationships with patients or clients. It became law in Switzerland in 1934. In the 1930s with the rise of the Nazis in Germany, Switzerland became an important haven for the funds of people fleeing from the Nazis, especially Jews. In order to preclude any misuse of banking information by foreign agents of Germany, the Swiss government at that time decided to build bank secrecy into their law.

Swiss bank secrecy has been subject to criticism, especially since World War II; for some countries believe, or claim to believe, that the cover of Swiss bank secrecy is being employed by criminal elements to hide their activities from the eyes of the authorities of their own countries. It is also felt that the existence of Swiss bank secrecy allows citizens in many countries of the world to avoid their income-tax obligations. The avoidance or nonpayment of income tax is not regarded as a criminal offense in Switzerland. It seems probable that owing to increasing foreign pressure there will be slight modifications in the application of the Swiss bank-secrecy law. At present it can be suspended only if a court order is issued by a Swiss court in a case where a serious criminal offence is strongly suspected. It could well be that the Swiss authorities will permit readier access to bank records when there is a request by a foreign government to the Swiss government for cooperation in regard to suspected misuse of bank secrecy. But if such erosion of secrecy does occur it will probably be protracted over some years, and will still apply only to flagrant cases. It should be pointed out that bank secrecy applies in many countries in varying degrees. Switzerland is apparently the only one with such strict provisions for punishment of those who break it—which acts as a deterrent. But considerable secrecy exists (without benefit of such law) in such places as Panama, Singapore, Austria, and Lebanon and in much of Europe. In fact, almost every country offers some degree of secrecy.

Banque d'Affaires

French term employed for a bank that is normally concerned with long-term financing and participation in direct ownership of corporations, usually industrial ones. It is the French approximate equivalent of the British **merchant bank**.

Banque de France

Central bank of France. It was created at the instigation of Napoleon Bonaparte by government decree of January 18, 1800, when it was organized as a private institution under the supervision of the state with an original capital of thirty million francs. On April 15, 1803, it was granted the exclusive privilege of issuing notes for the district of Paris. This monopoly was extended to all departments of France in 1848. By the law of December 2, 1945, the Banque was formally nationalized, a decade after supervision of its activities by the French state had already become almost complete.

Barron's

Weekly newsmagazine published by the Dow-Jones Publishing Company. It is a sister publication of the *Wall Street Journal. Barron's* specializes in presenting analyses of investment situations and is not afraid to express strong opinions along with facts. It is probably the most powerful voice for free enterprise in the United States. Its editorial policy is separate from that of all other Dow-Jones publications.

Barron's Business Gauge

Index of business trends in the United States, published in *Barron's* magazine. It tends to present a more accurate picture than the production index given out by the Federal Reserve Board.

Barron's Confidence Index

Index published by *Barron's* magazine which is a figure representing the ratio between the yield on high-risk bonds. The theory is that it supposedly shows the thinking of big money and thus elite money minds. It is erratic in its predictive power and seems to work well when it works and not at all at other times. Some years its predictive power has been 100 percent, in other years zero. It can perhaps be said that it shows the thinking of the "big boys," and when it doesn't work then the "big boys" haven't a clue to what is happening either.

Barter

Trading by exchanging one commodity (or service) for another at a rate fixed at the time of the transaction. In primitive societies, and indeed in countries where there have been periods of violent currency debasement and/or hyperinflation, the barter system of trading has usually been resorted to. Money as the "middleman" for trading transactions is honest money only if it keeps the previously agreed value from one month to the next, e.g., if the same number of a given coin will buy so many sheep, cows, or bathtubs. When the money value fluctuates radically, its usefulness as a middleman is largely lost, so people sometimes prefer to trade directly one commodity for another. The basic difficulty with straight barter is that if you make shoes and wish to buy a cow, you have not only to find a man who owns a cow he wishes to sell, but also to find a man who owns a cow for sale who also wishes to buy shoes. This makes the system cumbersome. But in simple societies where needs are few, a straight barter system is adequate. Also, in times of financial chaos, the rigidity of the barter system is to be preferred to the extreme flexibility of a fluctuating currency. The desire for preservation of capital at *some* point overcomes the awkwardness of barter.

Basel Agreement

Agreement reached in 1967 between the major countries of the West and the United Kingdom regarding the repayment of advances that some countries had given to the U.K. in the sterling crisis of that year. Essentially, the Bank of England promised its creditor nations (at least those nations which had lent it money during that particular sterling crisis) that they would receive repayment based upon the U.S. dollar rate of £1 = $2.38 instead of upon the sterling rate. In other words, they would receive a guarantee against any other future loss which might result from any new sterling devaluation. The Basel Agreement was significant in being the first occasion that a major country agreed to a dollar guarantee on its debt to third countries.

Bear

Originally an American expression used on the stock exchange for a person who expects that the prices of securities will, on balance, go down. It can also be used with reference to a single stock of commodity.

The term "bear market" is employed to describe a situation on the stock or commodity exchanges in which falling prices predominate.

Bellwether Stock

Stock used as a tool for determining the next direction of the stock market. All markets have "leaders," or stocks that tend to move first, before the rest. The market analyst, over a period of time, detects which these stocks are and watches any changes in their movement pattern for an indication of the direction of the rest of the market. A bellwether stock usually moves about two or three weeks ahead of the market as a whole.

Beneficial Owner

Anglo-American term to describe the actual end owner, usually of a security but also of other types of property. The beneficial owner is the ultimate or final and true owner, regardless of appearances that may mask his ownership. The term is applied only to a natural person; it cannot be applied to a corporation. The term is generally unknown in continental Western Europe.

Beneficiary

Legally, the person named in a trust, an insurance policy, or in a will to receive certain income or assets under predetermined conditions, usually on the death of the benefactor.

Bermuda

A tax haven. Bermuda to date has more or less escaped the violent racial tension that has existed in the other Atlantic and Caribbean islands off North America. The climate is cool but mild, and generally very pleasant, ranging between 60 and 86 degrees, with rain falling mainly in brief showers. *Taxation*: There are no income tax or death duties. The specialty of Bermuda, as a tax haven, is its exempted company structure, whereby companies set up in Bermuda pay a flat fee of $480 per year regardless of size of activity. In addition they pay an initial stamp duty of 0.5 percent of the authorized share capital. For details write Registrar of Companies, Accountant General's Department, Hamilton, Bermuda. *Residency*: Visitors may stay in Bermuda for periods of up to six months. If you wish to stay longer, permanent residency must be applied for. Citizenship is similar to that in the Bahamas up to recently: you become a British subject with Bermudian status. As in the Bahamas, the cost of living is very high, because most essentials are flown or shipped in. Like most island tax havens, Bermuda does not penalize nonresident companies, but it has to obtain revenue from somewhere, and does so mainly from import duties. Most island tax havens are good places to set up nonresident companies but economically bad places to live.

Big Five

In British banking, the five largest English commercial banks: Midland Bank, Ltd.; Barclay's Bank, Ltd.; Lloyd's Bank, Ltd.; National Provincial Bank, Ltd.; and Westminster Bank, Ltd.

Big Three

In Swiss banking, the three largest banks: Swiss Bank Corporation, Swiss Credit Bank, and Union Bank of Switzerland.

Bill Brokers

Dealers in bills of exchange. Increasingly they have turned their activities to commercial paper, that is, to the marketing of relatively short-term financial instruments issued by corporations, usually by placing them with financial institutions.

Billion

In Europe one employs the term "billion" to denote one million million. In the United States one regards a billion as being one thousand million. In Europe the term "milliard" is employed to denote one thousand million.

Bill of Exchange

IOUs that circulate among merchants, traders, and banks. They are the oldest form of paper money and are essentially short term bills of credit, usually for periods up to one year. They are in effect paper money with a backing, not of gold, silver, or government promises, but of commodities—the goods of the merchants and traders who use them.

Bimetallism

A now outdated term denoting the existence of two metals as currencies of a country at the same time, for example gold and silver. The United States was on a bimetallic standard of gold and silver from 1792 to 1873, and to a degree from 1878 to 1900, when the gold standard came into full effect.

Black Market

Black markets are usually the outward manifestation of a government upsetting free markets. A black market develops in any goods or services when open access to a free market is denied to the consumer. There can be a number of reasons for such denial. War or severe drought or some other disaster may cause goods to become so scarce as to be almost unobtainable; hence a black market may develop that enables the black marketeer to charge exorbitant prices for what is in effect a cornered market. Another cause of black markets is restrictive laws, forbidding or limiting the traffic in certain goods. This has the disastrous effect, almost without fail, of not only driving the traffic in such goods underground but also of pushing prices up so high as to encourage a gangster element who create their own market and then exploit it. Drug traffic is a radical case in point. While most people will agree that drug traffic is bad, it is arguable that there would be fewer victims and fewer such crimes as theft and embezzlement to support the habit if the sale of drugs were made legal to those who had unfortunately become hooked on them (as has been done in Britain). It can be speculated that the price would fall, which would eliminate many of the thefts now needed to support the drug habit, and also that without "pushers" many people would never become drug addicts in the first place.

Block Sale

Sale of a large number of shares, with a net purchase price usually in excess of $100,000. Under the regulations of the New York Stock Exchange the commissions on block sales of securities in excess of $250,-000 are no longer subject to a regular tariff or schedule of commission fees but can be negotiated on a case-to-case basis with the brokerage firm involved.

Blowoff

Term used in technical analysis to describe the market action when a move within an intermediate trend, after some movement in an upward direction, continues upward sharply, often on abnormally heavy volume. It is considered a sign that a reversal is about to take place, that the current uptrend has outlived itself and has produced a "blowoff."

Blue Chip

A term of American origin, at first designating a chip off a blue stone —a chip or splinter off a diamond. The term was also adopted for high-value poker chips. Today it is employed in finance to describe the shares of absolutely first-class corporations—those which are large, have had a very good record of earnings and of paying dividends, and are usually old and extremely well established. One of the supposed strengths of blue-chip securities is that they will maintain their value better than the shares of other corporations in times of recession and even depression. This theory has not always proved correct, and it is highly doubtful whether it will prove so in the future.

Bond Broker

Broker dealing on the exchange who specializes in the buying and selling of bonds. He is often involved in determining the original pricing of new issues.

Bond. See **Corporate Bond**

Bonus

In the financial field, usually employed to describe the payment of a special or additional dividend. European companies especially pay out such extraordinary dividends to mark special occasions, such as an anniversary of the founding of the firm. The advantage of this mode of payment is that it does not set a precedent for future dividend payments. The market will regard a bonus payment as a one-time thing and consider that the following year one cannot expect anything more than the normal dividend. One can also speak of bonus shares, involving the issuing of share dividends to shareholders to mark a special occasion.

Book Profit

Term used in contrast to *realized profit*. If, for example, one buys a security at $100 and its price rises to $110 but one does not sell it, one refers to the difference, namely $10, as a book profit. This book profit becomes a realized profit when the security involved is actually sold at this price.

Book Value

Estimated value of an asset if it were to be sold at current market prices. The book value per share of a company is arrived at by subtracting from the total book value of all its assets the estimated amount of all its liabilities and dividing the remainder by the total number of shares issued and outstanding. Book-value figures should be regarded with severe skepticism since they are necessarily based on uncertainties—estimations and opinions—with regard to which even those best informed may fall into serious error.

Bourse

The French term for "purse," then for "money market"; used to denote any of the European stock exchanges. See also **Paris Bourse**.

Breakaway Gap

A term used to describe a certain stock movement in which, when on a chart a stock has been making a consolidation pattern of some type or other it suddenly breaks out of the pattern, so that the price jumps up, leaving a price "gap" on the chart.

BREAKAWAY GAP

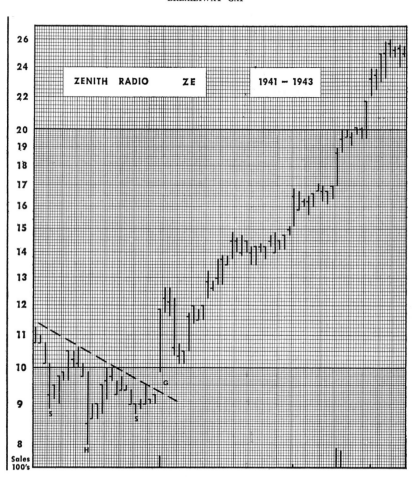

Breakaway Gap marked by letter "G"
Chart courtesy John Magee, Inc.

Bretton Woods

A town in New Hampshire where, between July 1 and July 22, 1944, the most famous monetary conference in modern times took place. The resulting Bretton Woods Agreement laid the foundation for both the **International Monetary Fund** and the **International Bank for Reconstruction and Development**. The participants in this conference were nations that had allied themselves against Germany, Italy, and Japan in World War II. Since then almost all nations of the world, except the Communist countries, have become members of the two organizations formed at that time.

Britain. See United Kingdom

Broadening Top

Chart formation that manifests itself as three peaks at successively higher levels and two intermediate lows, with the second lower than the first. The broadening-top formation is considered indicative of a fast-approaching market reversal.

BROADENING TOP FORMATION

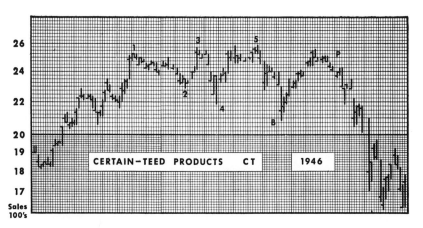

Chart courtesy John Magee, Inc.

Brokers

Salesmen of the stock exchanges. They are not advisers, even though they do give advice. If they follow the rule book, the advice they give tends to be standard advice formulated by their house analysts. The average brokerage house in the United States employs analysts to assess and predict the stock market, and their assessment is passed along to all brokers for transmission to their customers. The broker is also within his own area when he weighs this advice within the context of his customer. If his relationship with his customer is good, he will know if the customer can live with a high-flyer stock or if he prefers blue chips. However, it must never be forgotten that a broker gets paid on the *amount* of stock he buys and sells, *not* on whether or not he makes a profit for his client. Therefore even some brokers with great integrity will sometimes tend to want an account to keep turning over, rather than allowing stocks to sit for the longer term. One must bear this in mind when hearing or reading brokerage-house advice. Technically the word "broker" denotes only those who are personally members of a stock exchange, which normally means they own a partnership in a brokerage firm. They employ salesmen who are correctly called **account executives** (see) but whom the public calls "brokers."

Brussels

The capital of Belgium and also the capital of the EEC (European Economic Community), loosely called the Common Market. The importance of Brussels is more that of the administrative center of the European Common Market than of a financial center per se. Brussels has never developed the stature of a Frankfurt, Amsterdam, Zurich, Paris, or London in the financial realm. The stock exchange is of a rather limited scope in that only a very few international companies are listed on it, such as Petrofina, the oil group; Wagon-Lit, the railroad-car and catering group; and the various banks of Belgium such as the Société General and Banque Lambert. The Belgian franc has never developed into an international currency. Whereas there are major Eurocurrency markets in Eurodollars, Eurosterling, Euromarks, Euroguilders, Euro Swiss francs, and even Euro French francs, no international money market in Belgian francs has developed. However, in the economic sphere Belgium is of great importance, since it is the home not only of the commission of the EEC but also of many international trade associations, manufacturing associations, and European lobbies, representing many types of industrial, financial, and commercial groups, which have established themselves in the vicinity of the administration of the Common Market itself.

Increasingly Brussels has also become the administrative center for multinational corporations. Many of these have shifted their headquarters from Switzerland to Brussels because of the difficulties they have had in getting work permits in Switzerland, and also because they prefer to be situated in the "capital of Europe" in view of the prospects of the European Economic Community. This trend towards Brussels as an administrative capital for multinational companies, especially those of American origin, has attracted international banks (again heavily American) that have increasingly been establishing branch operations or buying up subsidiaries in Belgium and usually locating their headquarters in Brussels. In the future Brussels will increase in importance as a financial center, but even so will probably continue to be in the second rank of European financial capitals.

Bucket Shop

A type of brokerage house that, when operating under SEC law, is no longer allowable in the United States. If a client placed an order for buying shares of a stock that the bucket shop thought would go down, by *not placing* the order with a stock exchange (thus booking the "bet" themselves) they could take directly from the client the amount of points the stock dropped. In the days when bucket shops were at their height, this was very possible, for the bucket shop allowed its clients to trade on a very high leverage margin. With the client only putting up a small percentage of the amount of the stock money, the stock had only to drop a little for the client to be "sold out" because of a margin call; and if no transaction had taken place the bucket shop could pocket the entire amount advanced to it for the supposed purchase. The bucket shops were also the place where straight wagers on stock movements were made (no stock was bought or sold, merely a wager was made on the next direction of a particular stock). The term "bucket shop" is also loosely applied to telephone pressure selling of unlisted securities by hard-sell salesmen.

Budget

A forecast, usually covering the period of one year, of the expected income and expenses of a person or corporation. Often, especially in recent years, companies make attempts to forecast income and expenses over a much longer period—three or five years or even a full decade ahead. In those instances one usually refers to a "long-term plan" instead of a "budget," the latter being restricted to short periods.

Building Societies

British term for institutions that accept deposits from the public and give a high rate of interest in order to attract the money with which to finance home loans, mortgages, and property purchase. They are the British equivalent of American Savings and Loan Associations.

Bull

Stock-market term for somebody who expects to see a general rise in prices on the stock or commodity markets. One therefore speaks of a "bull market" when prices are in general on the rise. The term can be used for a single share or commodity as well as for the entire market or any group within the market.

Bullion

Gold or silver when in metallic bar or ingot form and not fashioned into coins, ornaments, etc. The term "bullion" technically applies strictly to the chemical makeup of the refined metal, i.e., the percentage of pure gold and/or silver versus impurities in the alloy. (See also **Karat**.)

Bundesbank

Central bank of West Germany, in Frankfurt, it is the successor to the German Reichsbank established in 1875. The Reichsbank, a central bank organized along the usual European lines, had exclusive banking power vested in itself. Following the military defeat of Germany in 1945, the Reichsbank was put into liquidation. Under the guidance of the occupying powers, especially that of the United States, the entire banking system of West Germany was reorganized along decentralized lines, the example followed being that of the U.S. Federal Reserve system. The states of West Germany received independent (especially *politically* independent) local central banks, along the lines of the Federal Reserve Districts in the United States. The Bundesbank (it was originally called Bank Deutsche Laender) became the central bank of these various State Central Banks, its capital being subscribed equally by them. All this was finally regulated in July 1957.

As a result of the remarkable industrial development in West Germany following World War II and of the West German government's success in containing inflation, the German mark (Deutsche mark) issued by the German Bundesbank developed into one of the hardest currencies in the world. This situation caused, especially during 1965–1972, vast amounts of money to be transferred into West Germany by foreigners who sought the safety and stability of its currency. The consequences have often been undesirable, and more than once voices have been raised suggesting that the Bundesbank should reject the ultra free-enterprise policies of the past and introduce controls, even stringent foreign-exchange controls, in order to protect Germany from misuse of its currency by foreign investors and especially speculators. The Bundesbank, however, has always rejected such demands, and in fact continues to be probably the strongest force in the entire European Economic Community favoring free capital movements. It remains violently opposed to the development of *Devisenbewirtschäftung* (total exchange control) such as that which existed in the 1930s when, as a result of foreign-exchange control, multiple exchange rates, competitive devaluations, and the like, Europe and the world became totally compartmentalized into separate monetary entities.

Business Cycles

Periodic movements between prosperity and recession of the general economy of a country or a group of countries. There are various types of business cycles. The shortest one is known as the "kitchen cycle," and lasts approximately eighteen months. This particular type of cyclical movement develops from the buildup and then depletion of inventories by business. The longest cycle that has been positively identified has been named after its discoverer, Nikolai D. Kondratieff, and lasts ap-

proximately twenty-seven years. There are also various types of intermediate business cycles of varying lengths that interact to produce a
general type of business cycle normally lasting seven years from peak
to peak and from trough to trough.

Buy Orders and Sell Orders

When buying or selling a stock on the American markets, you have a
choice. When you call up a broker, you can do more than just say
"Please buy (or sell) for me."

1. Market orders: These are the standard orders. You tell your broker
to buy or sell a certain stock for you "at the market." He in turn con-
tacts his man on the floor of the exchange, and the order is executed at
the price prevailing at the moment the order reaches the floor of the
exchange.

2. Limit orders: This way you make sure that, if your research has
told you a stock is a buy (or sell) at a certain price, you will not be
required to pay more (or get less) for it. Your broker will then only
buy at the price you specify or less, or sell at the price you specify or
more.

3. Immediate orders: Extensions of the limit order. You specify the
price at which you want the transaction to take place, and you also
specify that if the order cannot be filled at once it is to be canceled. This
is often a good idea, especially if you are the sort of person who forgets
you have limit orders in. You may have decided a stock is a buy at a
certain price and put in a limit order and if it "gets away from you"
(goes higher), you may then forget it. Then the price may drop badly
and suddenly days later you may find yourself in possession of a stock
which you no longer want and which is no longer a good buy. With
an immediate order you do not run this risk.

4. Scale orders: These are another variation of limit orders. You
instruct your broker to buy not just one lot but a number of lots. You
average down your price this way. For example, you might say "Buy
100 XYZ at 50 and 500 on a half-point scale down." This would mean
you would pick up the first 100 at 50 and (you hope) five additional
separate 100s each time the stock dropped half a point, i.e., at 49½, 49,
48½, and so on. You can also scale up.

5. Day orders (or week orders or month orders): These are canceled at the end of the time period specified if not executed by then. However, it should be noted that they expire at the end of the calendar (trading) week or month, not one month or week from the time you put the order in.

6. Good till canceled (G.T.C.) orders: The order remains in effect until you cancel it.

7. Market if touched (M.I.T.) orders: This is in many instances a more efficient way of placing a limit order. Often, if you are trading "close to the bone," your analysis of a stock and its turnaround point may be correct, but it bounces off the bottom so fast that your order was not executed. You then suffer the frustration of watching the stock go back up without you on the board. A market if touched order enables you to prove you are right and get in on it. When the stock touches your buy point, even if you cannot get *your* order executed at that price, the broker will pick it up for you "at the market" as near to the price as possible. Note that on this kind of order you must be very clear that if, for example, the stock hits your buy price and goes upwards *through* it, you may still consider the stock a buy. It could be that if the stock does not hesitate at the "buy" point, you would feel that your analysis would be invalidated; this is the danger of putting in specialized orders. *The safest orders are day orders and immediate orders. The rest must be treated with caution.*

8. Stop orders: These are to protect profits or to limit losses. They can be placed for several reasons. If you have a profit in a stock that is moving, say, in a zigzag line upwards within a range of three points, you might want to place a stop order four points below the market on the reasoning that at that price the uptrend would be violated and you want to get out. You then "trail" the stop sell order up under the stock, knowing that if you are out of touch with the market for any reason it will be executed should the stock fall (or rise in the case of a stop-buy over a short sale). It is often a good strategy to place a stop order on a stock the same day you buy it, to prevent any sudden move catching you off balance and to guard against any human tendency to postpone taking a loss when it really should be taken rather than risk having it grow into a more sizable one—one that you can't afford—or one that is simply poor trading tactics. This is probably sound procedure for *everyone*, except those who buy for the very long term and are willing to ride stocks down and (one hopes) back up. *A safe rule of thumb is to place an order to be stopped out automatically at 10 percent below one's*

*purchase price. (The percentage may vary with the price of the stock
or its volatility, but it shouldn't vary far.)*

9. *Mental stop orders:* These are the orders that are not placed with
your account executive (broker). They are kept in your head. The
rationale is that frequently stop orders are placed in accordance with
chart patterns or support levels. If many other people are watching the
stock, they will also be aware of these key support zones. If many orders
are on the specialists' books to sell at $39, then the abundance of such
orders will often force the stock through $39 to, say, $37; but then
when all the selling has dried up as a result of the big cleanout of orders,
the stock will bounce back, having made only a slight penetration of its
support within the day, and then close at $40. So the stop-loss order
would have taken you out unnecessarily. With only a *mental* stop you
can study the day's action: the high, the lowest price, the close, and the
volume. You can perhaps decide whether the stock really violated the
support level seriously from studying its closing price. If you decide
that a violation *was* serious, with the closing below your mental stop,
then you can sell at market the next day. You will get less money in
such cases, but you will prevent being stopped out prematurely in many
other cases.

Call Money

Originally employed to define very short-term interbank loans that
were callable at any time, with return payment to be made immediately
upon a "call" for it. In recent practice such call money is now often subject to one day's notice. Another name sometimes employed for call
money is "overnight loans." Such short-term transactions are quite often
employed for window dressing. At the end of a reporting period when the
balance sheets will be published, banks go through certain transactions of
this type in order to build up the size of their balance sheet, or to change
the structure of their balance sheet on a very short-term basis. As a rule
call money is of little or no interest to private investors, since normally
they do not have access to this particular part of the money market.

Calls

Options to buy a stock. The investor, instead of buying or selling short
a stock at the market and then taking his chances, instead buys a call

option. This entitles him to buy a particular stock at any time during the option period (65, 95, or 190 days) at a fixed price known as the *striking price.* If the stock never reaches the striking price, he loses the price of the call. The special attraction of buying a call rather than the stock is that one gets far more leverage, for the initial price of a call

A TYPICAL CALL ADVERTISEMENT

is a lot less than that of an equivalent amount of stock. It also limits your loss. If the stock falls like a rock, you can lose only your call-option money, a modest sum in most cases. For example, on October 24, 1972, you could buy a ten-month call option on Texas Gulf Sulphur for $137.50 per hundred shares, when the stock was selling at 16 ⅛ at an option price of 20. So you could tie up $16,000 worth of stock for $137 and if it fell you could lose only the $137. If it rose above 20 you would exercise the option at 20 and be buying it "below the going market price" at that time. These call options are listed in ads by put-and-call dealers in the *Wall Street Journal* (inside back page) every day. (See also **Puts** and **Straddle**.)

Cape Delivery

Term used mainly for South African stocks to denote where the stocks are registered. In general, South African stocks are either London delivery or South African delivery (Cape delivery).

Capital Appreciation

Appreciation (i.e., increase) in value of a capital asset.

Capital-Gains Tax

Tax on the profit from the sale of a capital asset, usually a security. If an investor buys a share of a corporation for $100 and later sells it for $150, the capital-gains tax will be applied to the $50 differential. The capital-gains tax stands in contrast to income tax, which is applied on the running income a person receives either as a result of his employment or as the result of his ownership of property. Income tax would be applied to the dividend an investor receives from the shares he owns, and to the interest he receives on his holdings of bonds. In most countries the tax on capital gains is much lower than that on income. The reason is that most governments seek to encourage private persons to invest in public corporations to promote the overall growth of the economy.

Capitalist

Term applied to either a system or group of people who are identified with the economic way of life we today term free enterprise. A Capitalist (or Capitalism) today is generally in contrast to a Communist (or Communism). The heart of the capitalistic system is private ownership, in opposition to the system of public or state ownership which forms the basis of both the Communist and socialist systems. The epitome of the capitalist system is a man who is willing to put his capital at risk in an enterprise in the hope that it will succeed and that the return on his capital will make it worthwhile to him.

Capitalization

Conversion of an asset into the capital of a corporation. Usually capitalization involves the conversion of money in some form. However, the term is also employed in regard to putting on the balance sheet as an asset something that has value but is intangible. For instance, Rolls-Royce capitalized its R and D (research and development) in various types of aircraft jet engines in the hope that ultimately the value of such research would come back to the corporation in the form of receipts from sales of the engines. In this case, as in many others, the practice led to the collapse of the corporation, since in a time of liquidity squeeze these are types of capitalized assets that cannot be exchanged for cash.

Capital Levy

Tax on capital. In Anglo-Saxon tradition (that is, in the United States, Canada, or the United Kingdom), taxes are generally restricted to levies on *income, sales,* and (where communities are concerned) *property.* But never is the tax imposed on the capital of either natural persons or corporations. This stands in contrast to the practice in many other parts of the world, especially Western Europe, where it is quite normal for the capital of a corporation and a natural person to be taxed. There, a person who has assets of, say, one million francs, with these assets being in the form of property, shares and bonds, cash in bank, etc., could have a tax levied on this capital. Normally this tax is relatively small, for example ¼ or ½ of 1 percent per annum.

Capital Market

Financial market in which long-term loans are made. Although there is no strict definition of where the money market stops and the capital market takes over, one generally refers to capital-market transactions if maturities of five years and longer are involved. The chief instruments involved in transactions in the capital market are bonds and shares.

Capital Preservation. See **Preservation of Capital**

Carat. See **Karat**

Cartel

Grouping of companies for the purpose of controlling markets. The most famous cartel after World War I was I.G. Farben of Frankfurt, Germany. This cartel embraced all the major chemical producers of that country, who banded together on a worldwide basis and as a result gained dominance in many markets. The advantages of a cartel are that it allows members to eliminate any competition among themselves on the one hand and on the other to gang up on other companies, usually smaller companies or groups in the field, and put them out of business. They thus control prices. Many countries have made cartels illegal. The United States has led the way in this regard with the introduction and implementation of very stringent antitrust laws. However, some countries, such as Switzerland, do not regard cartels as illegal or even as unhealthy groupings. In fact, in that country their formation is encouraged by the government, which feels that in some instances cartels will enable Swiss industry to compete in world markets where otherwise this would not be possible.

Cash Flow

The flow of funds during a specific period of time, normally the twelve months of a financial year. It is gross income plus depreciation, and must not be confused with income. The sources of cash flow are normally the following: net profits, the new issue of securities, sale of land, factories, equipment, or other assets. The employment of such cash is summarized as follows: dividends paid out, new investments in plant and equipment, repayment of debt. Study of the cash flow is extremely important in judging the ability of a corporation to finance itself. If analysis indicates that the corporation is able to continue to build up its productive assets as well as to pay out a decent dividend to its shareholders and that it is able to do this strictly out of the cash flow generated from profits, it signifies sound financial health. Conversely, if a corporation in order to finance its current affairs and future development is being forced to continually issue new shares or bonds or make other new borrowings, this is a negative factor that casts doubts on the long-term viability of the firm.

Cayman Islands

A group of three islands lying 200 miles northwest of Jamaica. Despite United Kingdom restrictions on sterling outflow, they continue to sell their tax-haven status. There is no income tax, capital-gains tax, property tax, or inheritance tax. A Cayman company requires three shareholders, none of whom need be residents. The cost of setting up a company is 1/20 of 1 percent of capital, with a minimum of £25 and a £2 stamp duty; there is an annual fee of 1/40 of capital, with a minimum of £12.10 annually. An annual general meeting must be held, but not necessarily in the Caymans. An exempted company can obtain an undertaking from the government that it will not be subjected to tax for a fixed number of years, usually fifteen. An exempted trust can obtain a guarantee against future taxes of up to fifty years from date of trust. Stamp duty is payable on issue of shares at the rate of 2 new pence per share having a par value of less than £50 (if over £50, 10 new pence per share). Because of political stability, a modern companies law, and no taxation, there is considerable interest in the Caymans, and their tax-haven business in all its aspects is almost doubling annually.

Central Banks

Very different from the commercial banking institutions familiar to the man in the street, central banks are "guardians" of the finances of the countries in which they are located. Each is, if you like, the monarch of its country's money. It can be said that, since every central bank is run by appointees, not elected members, no country, even in the free world, is an *economic* democracy—we are all to greater or lesser degree living in economic dictatorships. In theory central banks are servants, not masters, of governments. But since they also have their own international fraternity, the whole system is very much a twilight zone, with the general public not really certain just how much power the wielders of international finance hold.

Certificate of Deposit

Document issued by a bank stating that it owes a depositor the amount on the face of the certificate, which is usually issued to him at the time the bank receives his funds. It is really just a temporarily frozen savings account. It draws more interest than a regular savings account because the bank can keep it for a known (and long) period. Certificates of deposit are always called by their initials (CD). Normally CDs are issued only to major depositors, and they usually are for $100,000 or more, though $25,000 is acceptable in some banks. A CD is usually a bearer instrument that can be sold in the after market. CDs are always issued for specific periods, ranging from one month up to as long as two years. Essentially a CD states that the bank, at the end of the given period, will repay the capital plus interest to the certificate holder upon presentation.

Certificate Check

Term, especially in the United States, for a check whose validity has been certified by the bank on which it was drawn. The bank stands behind the check and will cash it under any circumstances.

Change

Word used throughout the world for an office dealing in foreign exchange, i.e., trading in foreign currency. The biggest moneychangers are Deak & Co., Inc., and the Perera Co., Inc., which have offices around the world.

Channel Islands

Eight islands in the English Channel between England and France, constituting a tax haven. They are British territory. With the exception of the island of Sark (which has no income tax), the income-tax rate is 20 percent. There are no capital-gains or withholding taxes or estate duty in any of the Channel Islands, and no death duties or surtax. Companies registered in the Channel Islands pay a corporation tax of a flat £200 per year. From a British point of view, the chief advantage of the Channel Islands is that they are about the only sterling tax haven left that is within United Kingdom's exchange control. While the Channel Islands would never have grown economically the way they have done without the influx of offshore money, they do not want to encourage avoidance of tax. It is therefore impossible for new residents to set up companies openly for tax-avoidance purposes. There is a big market in old companies (shells). There are no secrecy laws in the Channel Islands.

Chart Paper. See **Arithmetical Graph Paper**

Charts and Chart Reading

Much controversy rages in the field of market analysis between those known as "fundamentalists" and those known as "chartists"; in other words, between those who use basic market facts and figures and company reports and the like to determine when and what to buy or sell, and those who keep and study charts of stocks and who rely completely on the "patterns" the charts make. There are a number of recognized patterns in stock charts, such as head and shoulders, rising wedges, triangles, etc., that have specific meanings for chartists. Good chart reading is an art, not a science. It's like painting. Anyone can be taught to put paint on a canvas or to read a chart, but great painting and successful chart reading are the exception rather than the rule. *The best analysts tend to use both approaches.*

A chart pattern is a configuration showing a known action on the part of market traders. If in an unusually high number of cases in the past such action has almost always led to the same result, then in the future it is reasonable to assume that when the configuration appears again it will resolve itself similarly to last time, the time before, and the time before that. However, people are never totally predictable and thus chart patterns cannot be treated like a magic horoscope of some stock or commodity. Still, there are undoubtedly tendencies for a stock to behave in certain ways. An extremely good book explaining the various chart patterns is *Technical Analysis of Stock Trends,* by Robert D. Edwards and John Magee (John Magee, Inc., 360 Worthington Street, Springfield, Mass. 01103; 1966).

Chicago School

Label for an economic theory born in Chicago. It contends that the fundamental equation determining the macro-economic (see **Macro Economics**) path of a national economy involves money supply and the velocity of money turnover.

City

"The City" is the financial center of London, a relatively small part of London in which all the major national and international banks as well as the various securities and commodities exchanges are concentrated. It is also sometimes referred to as "the Square Mile."

Clearinghouse

Term used for institutions that handle settlements among the banks of a financial community. It is not necessary for every bank each day to sort out and present the items requiring payment to or from every other bank (checks, etc.). Rather the bank can send all these items to a clearinghouse that groups them and provides the facilities for settlements with other banks on a net basis.

Closed-End Investment Company

This stands in contrast to a mutual fund. Whereas a mutual fund is constantly issuing new participation certificates to new investors, a closed-end investment company issues its shares to the investing public the same as any other corporation. In other words, it makes a once and for all (or periodic) issue of shares, just as any other public company might do. Closed-end investment companies, however, are not involved in the running or even financing of any specific company or business. They employ the funds provided to them by the investing public for investment in the shares of public corporations, and often become major shareholders in these corporations. Some closed-end investment companies specialize in specific fields. For example, American South African Corporation specializes in the shares of gold mines in South Africa. Generally the shares of closed-end investment corporations sell at a discount running from 10 to 20 percent under their **book value** (see). One reason is that large-block share holdings are often involved, so that the investment community takes into consideration the fact that the cash generated by sale of them all at once would probably be less than their listed asset value. In other words, the portfolios of these companies probably could not be sold except at a discount from current market prices because of the large size of the blocks of stock involved.

Collateral Trust Bonds

Bonds backed by collateral, usually other bonds and stocks in subsidiary companies.

Commercial Banks

Banking institutions whose main business is the acceptance of deposits from the general public and the making of loans to the business community.

Commercial Paper

Instrument of debt that is eligible for discounting in financial markets. Commercial paper is usually issued by large corporations with excellent credit ratings. They normally involve relatively short periods of repayment, i.e., between ninety days and three years. There is a very active market in commercial paper in such centers as New York and London. Normally the countries of continental Europe do not employ this type of financial paper.

Commodity

Generally, a raw material, usually either of agricultural origin or a mining product. Commodities are of many varieties, ranging from butter to zinc. A list of commodities traded in the U.S.A. is much longer than most people realize. *Foods:* coffee, flour, potatoes, cocoa, sugar, eggs, buttter, frozen orange juice, broilers, pork bellies, hogs, steers, pepper. *Grains and Feed:* wheat, corn, oats, rye, barley, rapeseed, soybeans, flaxseed, bran, linseed meal, cottonseed meal, soybean meal. *Fats and*

Oils: cottonseed oil, corn oil, soybean oil, peanut oil, coconut oil, lard, tallow, linseed oil. *Textiles and Fibers*: cotton, print cloth, sheeting, burlap, wool, rayon. *Metals*: steel scrap, copper scrap, lead, zinc, tin, aluminum, quicksilver, silver, silver coin, platinum. *Miscellaneous*: hides, gasoline, fuel oil, rubber, plywood, lumber.

How to open a commodity account: Most major stockbrokers also handle commodities. If you want to start trading in commodities, the easiest way is to ask your stockbroker to introduce you (by phone if you like) to someone in the firm's commodity department. No doubt the first thing the commodity broker will suggest is that you open an account, offering to send the opening papers. When you read through the forms you will probably be scared out of your wits; typically the more fainthearted drop the matter right there. Normally, you will be asked to sign a statement saying: "I am well aware that commodity trading involves a highly speculative activity in thinly margined and fast-moving markets," or, "I am aware that price movements in commodity markets are subject to sharp up and down swings and realize that any sharp price fluctuation may result in a severe loss of my capital," and that "I will in no way hold X Brokerage Company responsible for losses." Further, you will definitely be asked to sign a statement authorizing the broker to sell you out without *prior demand or notice to you* should the broker regard your cash margin as inadequate for his protection. They will also no doubt ask you to provide financial references. Having seemingly signed your life away and returned these documents, you are almost in business. The next step will be to decide exactly what you want to trade in, to what extent, and then send the broker the appropriate cash margin.

Commodity trading units and margin requirements: Each commodity exchange has specific trading units, i.e., minimum standard quantities of the commodity in which you can trade. Example: the quantity in silver futures contracts on the New York Commodity Exchange is 10,000 oz; in Chicago it is 5,000 oz. Let us assume you want to buy a December 1973 silver future contract in New York, and the price is $2 per ounce. It means you would be contracting for a December 1973 delivery of 10,000 oz. of silver, having a total value of $20,000. Your broker would ask you to put up between 10 percent and 20 percent cash margin

($2,000 to $4,000) before executing the order. These funds would go into a blocked account. Similarly, should you move into trading other commodities, such as wheat or sugar, in all cases you will have to deal in standard trading units. It is important you become familiar with these units. They are listed below for the popular commodities:

Commodity	Contract Unit	Approx. Current Contract Value	Approx. Margin Per Contract
Silver NY	10,000 oz	$20,000	$2,000
Silver Chi	5,000 oz	$10,000	$1,000
Platinum NY	50 oz	$ 7,500	$ 750
Copper NY	25,000 lbs	$12,500	$1,250
Cocoa NY	30,000 lbs	$10,000	$1,000
Sugar NY	112,000 lbs	$10,000	$1,000
Wheat Chi	5,000 bus	$10,000	$1,000
Corn Chi	5,000 bus	$ 7,000	$ 700
Pork Bellies	25,000 lbs	$12,500	$1,250

This table is not complete, but it should be apparent that the average contract value is around $10,000, requiring a cash margin of about $1,000. The quotes you read always relate to price per unit of quantity, not to the contracts. Thus March sugar 8.52 means the price is just over 8½ cents per pound. If December wheat is quoted at 2.15, it means $2.15 per bushel. To get the market value of the contract you hold, simply multiply the unit price by the number of units per contract, e.g., for sugar 8.52 cents times 112,000; for wheat, $2.15 times 5,000. You will note that each futures month normally has a different price. Thus December 1972 wheat might be quoted at $2.15 per bushel, March 1973 at $2.20, and July 1973 at $2.25. As a rule, the further into the future, the higher the price, but there are many exceptions.

The nature of futures commodity contracts: As a private commodity speculator, you always deal in futures. A future is a legal contract under which you agree to either *take* delivery (if you go long) or *make* delivery (if you go short) of the agreed amount of that commodity (like 10,000 oz. of silver, or 112,000 lb. of sugar) in a stated month in the future. This contract is as legal and binding as any other type of commercial contract. But (and this is a strategic "but") a commodity speculator never lets his contracts mature. He covers, *or* gets out of his contract by entering into a second contract for exactly the same amount, but on the other side. In other words, if he originally *bought* 10,000 oz. of silver for delivery in December 1973, he covers by *selling* 10,000 oz. of silver for delivery in December 1973 through the *same* broker. He might "cover" in this fashion one day or three months after the original purchase, but in any case he would do so prior to the December 1973 delivery date. Obviously the later the delivery month (e.g., twelve months into the future instead of just one month), the more maneuverability a speculator has.

Selling short: Most investors are accustomed to working exclusively on the "long" side, because of their experience in the stock market. To go short on stocks is sometimes awkward as you must borrow and await an uptick, and some brokers are unhelpful to customers on the short side. Not so in commodities. It is just as easy to go short as long in this market. In fact, for every speculator who goes long on a commodity future, there *has* to be a matching one who goes short, unless the seller is an actual commodity producer, or a merchant selling existing inventory of the producers' expected crop in advance. Here is a typical short: A speculator expects the price of wheat to drop in 1973. So he *sells* one May 1973 contract at $2.15 a bushel (worth a total of $10,750) in the hope that between then and next spring he will be able to buy those 5,000 bushels of wheat (which he does not have) at a lower price. The potential profit would be the difference between his original selling price and his eventual purchase price; for example, if during the next weeks or months wheat *does* fall and he can purchase a May 1973 contract at $2 a bushel, the contract would only have a total cost of $10,000, leaving him a profit of $750. At this point his wheat position is now "closed out." So he can withdraw both his original $1,000 cash margin and this profit from his commodities account and take a three-day vacation in Hawaii.

Stop-loss orders: Continuing the example of the wheat short position, a speculator would enter a "stop loss" if he told his broker, at the time of the original sell order, to cover if the May 1973 wheat price rose to, say, $2.30. Then if the speculator was wrong on the trend of the market, his broker would *automatically* cover at $2.30, and his customer's loss would be restricted to $750. In theory this is a splendid approach to commodity trading as it limits losses from unexpected moves. But it often backfires. The price may jump right *over* a stop-loss limit; and before the broker's standing order gets executed, the price has zoomed further and the customer's total cash margin is gone. It can also boomerang thus: During the in-day trading the price might rise to $2.30, where the broker *must* cover, under the stop loss order. But by the day's end wheat may have retreated to $2.20 again, and a week later to $1.90. The speculator would have a $750 realized loss, instead of the $1,250 profit he would have made had he not placed an automatic stop. I suggest that you work with *mental* stops. This means that *you,* not your broker, note the price at which you want to get out to preclude further losses; when that point is reached, you just pick up the phone and tell your broker to cover immediately. If you base your decision on closing prices, not intraday, you will save many situations that would have been lost under a rigid stop order.

Margin calls: Let us stick to the wheat example, assuming you went short on one Chicago wheat contract at $2.15, putting up a cash margin of $1,000, and placed a no stop-loss order. If, contrary to your expectations, May 1973 wheat rose in price to $2.30, your margin cover would no longer be 10 percent but only 2 percent. At this point your broker would get into a highly nervous condition and both phone and wire you, saying that either you "fill up" your margin by sending an additional $1,000 pronto or he will sell you out. Another $1,000 margin would make you "safe" from his standpoint, even if wheat's price rose another 20 cents. But from your standpoint, it could mean you were throwing good money after bad, rather than admit you were wrong. My advice: think very hard before you meet a margin call. Statistically the odds are 2 to 1 in favor of a price trend continuing in the same direction.

Commissions: Commodity brokerage commissions are not handled like stock-market commissions. First, they are not billed when the original order is executed, but only after the trade has been completed, i.e., after the long or short position has been closed out by an additional transaction. The commission charged then is for both purchase and sale. The term used is "round turn commission." Such commissions are amazingly low, e.g., on a New York silver contract just $45; on a

Chicago pork-belly contract, $30. It means you can do a high volume of in-and-out trading, even during a single trading session, and not see your profits eaten up by commissions. This is unique in the investment world.

Leading commodity brokers. Both Bache and Merrill Lynch offer complete services. Two lesser-known companies in this field appear to offer personalized services: Heinold Commodities, Inc., 222 Riverside Plaza, Chicago, and Reynolds Securities Inc., 140 Broadway, New York (Edward Edelstein).

Common Market. See European Economic Community

Common Stock

Stock held *in common* with other owners of the company. Every corporation has common stock, whether it is a private or a public company (i.e., whether it has "gone public" or not).

Communism

In the economic sphere, that type of system prevalent in Eastern Europe, Central Asia, and China based upon the philosophy of Karl Marx and involving public ownership and management of all productive facilities. The Communist system stands in contrast to the Capitalist system, which is based upon private ownership of the productive facilities of a nation. An oddity is the fact that most people in those countries which we generally think of as Communist do not use that term in referring to themselves. Rather they speak of themselves as socialists, since under the master's theory the state of Communism is one of perfection that has not yet been achieved and will be reached only after many successive stages of advancement.

Consols

Bonds issued by the British government. Originally consols were un-dated, in that there was no specific date given for their repayment. In recent times consols have been issued with specific repayment dates.

Contingent Liabilities

These are potential problems, especially in the case of banks. They are usually not listed directly on the balance sheet, but rather in a form often described as "below the line." They are usually guarantees issued by the company, which considers it improbable that it will ever have to stand good for. An investor, however, is well advised to scrutinize such contingent liabilities. If there are many of these or if some are of a rather peculiar nature, it may well mean that the financial status of the corporation is not nearly so healthy as the record otherwise would indicate.

Contocurrent Account

The word "contocurrent" is used in German-speaking parts of the world, (e.g., West Germany and most of Switzerland) to describe what is known in the Anglo-Saxon countries as a checking account.

Contrary Opinion

A market theory based on the concept that the "mass man" is generally wrong. The idea is that in money and market trends the first people to make a move have good reason for doing so—let us say that they buy because they see future increased earnings in a stock. The stock moves up a few points. Slowly, more and more people see the stock moving and get on the bandwagon. By the time the mass public see the move and get in, then either the stock is overpriced or the original reason for its move has long since gone and the "insiders" are already getting out, leaving the "little man" carrying the can. Humphrey B. Neill of Pawlet, Vermont, produces a market letter based on this concept: when the crowd moves, it is fairly safe to move in the opposite direction. As Goethe put it, "I find more and more it is well to be on the side of the minority, since it is always the more intelligent."

Convertibility

Condition in which one currency can be freely exchanged for another without government restrictions. Very few currencies are totally convertible. Among these are the Swiss franc, the West German mark, and the Canadian dollar. Almost all other currencies, including the American dollar, are not freely convertible into other currencies because governments have imposed restrictions. The term is also sometimes used to mean "convertible into gold," but one should use the full phrase and not assume that convertibility by itself has this special meaning.

Convertible Bond

A bond that can be transformed or converted into common shares at a price or rate specified upon issuance of the bond. This is done as an inducement to buy the bond, since a rise in the shares offers a bonus potential.

Convertible Preferred Stock. See Preference Shares

Corner

One speaks of a corner when a group of investors has managed to gain control or to monopolize trade of a given commodity. Especially in the nineteenth century in the United States, groups often got together to form a corner, and it was possible for them to withhold the product (e.g. corn, cocoa, or whatever) from the market, thus forcing the price higher and higher. A corner was especially effective in a market in which large short positions had been built up by speculators who had invested because they thought that the price of the commodity was going to fall. They would sell short, that is, they would sell contracts for that commodity even though they did not have any physical ownership of it. At the end of the contract period it became necessary for them to produce what they had sold. If a corner had been established, it became impossible for them to acquire the commodity without paying exorbitant prices to the group holding the corner.

Corporate Bond

Vehicle (or method) through which a company borrows money. It issues a medium- or long-term note (bond) in which it guarantees repayment at a specified future date and guarantees payment of pre-determined amounts of interest at stated intervals. If a company does not or cannot make the interest payments on its bonds, it can be forced into bankruptcy. Unlike dividends on a stock, payments on a bond are mandatory. They are not dividends depending on profits but interest payments on a debt. When you buy a bond, you are not buying part of the company as you do when you buy stock; you are merely lending the company money. You won't ever get a share of the profits should the company do exceptionally well; on the other hand, if the price of the shares declines badly, you still get paid. Even if the company goes broke, the bondholder fares better than the shareholder (before the latter gets anything, the bondholders must be paid as nearly in full as possible).

Corporation

Generally, a business entity having only limited liability and issuing shares. A corporation is quite different from a partnership or a sole proprietorship or a co-op type of institution. The corporation was a British invention and is of fundamental importance in the capitalistic system, for it is the corporation which attracts capital and turns it to productive uses in ways that have become an integral part of the Western world.

Costa Rica

Though not a tax haven in the normal sense of the word, Costa Rica does have possibilities for the nonresident. The tax advantage is that you are taxed only on income from Costa Rican sources. A foreigner who establishes his domicile in Costa Rica and obtains his income abroad will not be subject to Costa Rican tax.

Coupons

Pieces of paper normally attached to a bond. A bondholder clips these coupons off, usually at the end of a twelve-month period, in order to present them to his bank, who gives them to the issuer of the bond and receives the interest due on the bond for that period of time.

Courtage

Term throughout the European continent for brokerage fees.

Crawling Peg

Theory of automatic currency adjustment that has been put forward to cope with recent monetary crises. The theory is that, instead of major crises and devaluations every decade or so, some system whereby a currency is devalued a small amount every year could be used. This theory presupposes that inflation and the necessity for devaluation from time to time is incurably inherent in any monetary system. The notion is that the currency should "crawl" weekly or at slightly longer periods according to a present formula, possibly based on the moving average of its depreciation for the past year.

Crossed Checks

When two diagonal lines are drawn across the face of a check, the amount involved can be paid only into an account at a bank. In other words, the person who presents the check cannot withdraw the amount as cash. This device is very commonly used in Britain and in the former British colonies. Americans usually find it an irritating custom, for it places the decision on how the check is to be paid on the maker of the check, not the recipient.

Currency Bands

Area, or band, within which a currency is allowed to fluctuate on both sides of its official parity. In the Washington Smithsonian Agreement of 1971, it was agreed that such bands would be set at 2.25 percent each side of the parity. Let us take the pound sterling to demonstrate how this works in practice. The central rate or parity of sterling in terms of American dollars was then set at $2.6057. It was to be allowed to drop in value as low as 2.5471 American dollars or to rise as high as 2.6643. These two points are the upper and lower intervention points, that is, the points at which the Bank of England is obligated to intervene in order to maintain the value of its currency within the permissible fixed range. This means, of course, that under current rules the *total* range for movement in the international value of a currency is 4.5 percent. (See also **Currency Parities**.)

Currency Blocs

A group of countries that use a common currency, e.g., the sterling bloc and the French franc bloc. In the sterling bloc or sterling area, sterling is not only the currency of the United Kingdom but is also used by many former colonies in Africa and other areas of the world as their international means of exchange. These countries maintain their international reserves either in the form of gold or sterling deposits. These sterling funds are normally deposited in London, where they draw good interest.

Currency Futures

For most people the world of currency futures has remained totally unexplored. It is widely regarded as an esoteric area of international finance, restricted to sophisticated bankers and treasurers of large multinational corporations. This need not be so. In today's monetary climate, in this new era of constantly fluctuating exchange rates, it is, in our judgment, prudent for all private investors to become acquainted with the techniques of operation with currency forward contracts. Currency futures can be an easy way to protect one's assets from erosion through devaluation. They can, for the more daring, also be a vehicle for making capital gains on a highly leveraged basis. In this area of finance, like all others, there is no one-way street. There are pitfalls that can cost an investor money, sometimes lots of it, if he does not correctly assess his exposure. For some reason, operations in currency futures have been identified with evil little gnomes, trying to make a fast buck at the expense of a hard-working, diligently honest world. To sell General Motors short is O.K., but to sell the dollar or pound short is unpatriotic and/or seamy. This viewpoint is complete nonsense. Paper currencies are really nothing other than noninterest-bearing government securities. As an investor in these securities you have as much right to speculate in the specific market in which these securities are trading, namely the foreign-exchange market, as you have to speculate in RCA, on either the long or short side, on the New York Stock Exchange. If a farmer need feel no moral compunctions about selling his wheat in the commodities futures market in Chicago in order to guarantee the future value of his assets, so also no one who wants to guarantee the future value of his investment in cash dollars should feel any qualms about seeking insurance in the currency futures market in Zurich or Chicago.

Now to mechanics. We shall use the Swiss franc–U.S. dollar exchange situation as the basis for our analysis. The use of this relationship is deliberate, for it is in Switzerland that most people center their foreign-exchange operations. The reasons are many. Swiss banks are more familiar with transactions of this type than banks of any other nation. They deal in all currencies. They do not give you the raised-eyebrow treatment when you approach them on this subject such as you would almost certainly get from a banker in New Jersey. Swiss banks offer competitive rates, though you as a client must press for them. Most important, when you center your foreign-exchange operations with a Swiss bank you are working from a hard-currency base, the Swiss franc.

To see how the market works, let's go back to early 1971, when the spot rate of exchange was Swiss francs 4.30 = $1.00. (By "spot" one means the current cash-and-carry rate of exchange—here it means the rate you got then when you exchanged dollars for Swiss francs on the spot.) Let us assume that in March 1971 you decided it was time to protect your dollar assets against deterioration through devaluation. Let us further assume that you had one million dollars in assets in the United States, ranging from real estate to securities to Treasury-bills to cash in the bank. Let us finally assume that you also had a small nest egg in Switzerland, say 200,000 Swiss francs on time deposit. Rather than going through the time-consuming trouble and perhaps risk of liquidating all your dollar assets and shipping the proceeds off to Switzerland, you decided to "buy insurance" in the currency futures market. So you asked your Swiss bank to sell $1 million short, against the Swiss franc, on a six-month basis.

What does selling this $1 million short mean? It means that you are selling dollars (which you do not own) in Switzerland, to be delivered to the purchaser (a foreign or U.S. bank) six months from the date of contract. The contract you enter fixes the future selling price of your dollars in Swiss francs. It's as if you promised to deliver a ton of fresh strawberries to me in June, when they ripen, and we agree now that the price will be fifty cents a pound. Of course, right now you don't have any strawberries. But you anticipate that you will be able to grow them (or buy a ton from somebody else) prior to delivery time in June. And you hope that you will be able to grow or buy them at a cost under the fifty cents you have agreed to sell them for, to me, in June.

To go back to Swiss francs and the dollar: The forward selling rate for dollars against Swiss francs normally involves a discount where the dollar is concerned. Thus on March 3, although the spot rate offered was 4.30 Swiss francs = $1.00, the six-month forward rate (for delivery in September 1971) was 4.26 Swiss francs = $1.00. The contract you entered into on that date said the following: "I promise to deliver to you, Bank X, $1 million on September 3, 1971. You promise to pay me 4,260,000 Swiss francs for these dollars." It is as simple as that! So along came September 3, 1971, and with great joy you asked your Swiss bank to "cover" for you. The bank went into the spot market, bought dollars for you, and delivered them to Bank X, on your behalf. But in the meantime the Swiss franc had been *revalued*. As a result your bank could buy dollars for you at the new spot rate of 3.96 Swiss francs = $1.00. So you, through your agent (your Swiss bank), paid out 3,960,000 Swiss francs to buy $1 million, and then delivered the said $1 million immediately to Bank X. In a back-to-back transaction, under the terms of the contract you entered into on March 3, Bank X then paid you 4,260,000 Swiss francs for this same $1 million. You have just made yourself 300,000 Swiss francs (the prearranged selling price of SwFr 4,260,000 less the current covering cost of SwFr 3,960,000).

What about margin on these transactions? Well, in the case here, where you had 200,000 Swiss francs on deposit at a Swiss bank that set up forward exchange contracts for you, it is not at all improbable that the bank would have required no margin whatsoever. It might merely have asked that your funds be put on a fixed deposit basis with them for a period at least matching the period of your outstanding foreign-exchange contracts. In other cases they may seek to block 5 percent of the face amount of the currency contract (in our example, 5 percent of around four million Swiss francs) in a noninterest-bearing margin account.

Currency Parities

Under the international monetary rules laid down by the International Monetary Fund, currencies of all major countries of the world are fixed in terms of U.S. dollars. At the time of writing one U.S. dollar equals 2.87 Swiss francs; one U.S. dollar equals 2.396 Deutsche marks; one U.S. dollar equals 4.095 French francs. Prior to the joint float which began in 1973, these would have been central, fixed rates at which these currencies could be exchanged for an American dollar. However, the rates of exchange are allowed to fluctuate by 2.25 percent up or down from this central (or parity) rate. A currency devaluation or other revaluation is done in terms of parity. Thus, when the pound sterling was revalued in 1971 there was an official change in the parity from $2.40 to $2.6057. The new parities are registered with the International Monetary Fund and become the basis for future international currency transactions. In early 1973 the major European currencies formed a joint float against the dollar. This meant they were floating together as though they were a single currency. The pound and the lira, however, floated separately. Rigid parities are for the moment largely abandoned, but will doubtless return soon.

Cycles. See **Business Cycles**

Day Orders. See **Buy Orders and Sell Orders**

Debasement

Reduction of value of currency in circulation. This term was especially used when most currency in circulation was in the form of metal coin. Debasement occurred when the precious-metal content of such coins, for example gold and silver, was reduced in favor of a higher proportion of nonprecious metals such as lead or zinc. In modern times one refers to currency debasement as an effect of inflation where, as a result of ever-increasing prices, the purchasing power of currency is steadily reduced, and thus the currency is debased. A high rate of money-supply increase means instant debasement.

Debt

Money owed.

DEFLATION 64

Deflation

A contraction in the volume of available money or credit, resulting in a decline of the general price level. *Deflation* is the word employed in opposition or in contrast to *inflation*. Whereas under inflation a country experiences steadily and rapidly rising prices, under deflation exactly the opposite is true: prices fall. One of the key factors in determining whether an economy is inflationary or deflationary is the creation of money in circulation by the central government. In general one can say that increases in the supply of money at too rapid a rate produce inflation, while insufficient creation of money brings about deflation. Economists differ on the causes of inflation and deflation, but all must agree there is a link between these phenomena and money creation or contraction. The economists differ mainly on the size of the link.

De Gaulle

General Charles de Gaulle was the leader of the Free French forces in World War II and later President of France. He is no doubt the most important French figure of the twentieth century. He was known for his independent attitude in world politics and also for his promotion of the glory of France. In the economic field, de Gaulle was best known for his opposition to the United States on such issues as gold and the dollar deficits. He and his advisers strongly felt that gold should remain the basis for the world monetary system and that the dollar's role in international economics should be decreased to the greatest degree possible.

As the leader of the French people, he brought the French franc from being an international joke, with devaluations every couple of years, to being one of the strongest European currencies. He succeeded in stabilizing the franc in a way no French leader had done before him for many decades. Because of his consciousness of the statehood of France and her economic position, he felt antagonism to the dollar. While he was stabilizing the franc with disciplines imposed at home, he was forced, because of the international monetary system, to import the lack of discipline of the dollar, and so import its inflation. His preoccupation with a gold-backed currency was predicated on a desire for a national currency that was both sound and not dominated by an outside power. Neither of those points seems possible with a world currency system based on a steadily inflating United States dollar. Events have seemingly proved de Gaulle's fears justified and his goals laudable. History may show that his sound-money (based on gold) views were not radical— but rather that those who wanted a world founded on unbacked paper currency were the radicals.

Depreciation. See **Amortization**

Depression

An emotional word whose usage has been changed by politicians in the last forty years. In the strictly economic sense, *depression* denotes a period of economic stagnation, be it mild or severe. However in recent years it has generally been accepted that one should apply the term *recession* to mild, short-term business relapses, and save *depression* to refer to a more drastic longer business stagnation such as occurred in the 1930s. Apparently a rose by another name was deemed to be sweeter.

Depressions can be caused by two basic conditions. The first and most obvious one is a business slowdown which causes unemployment to rise and sales to drop, until you end up with a classic depression of the 1930s variety. In more recent years, depressions and recessions have tended to be caused purely by currency and inflationary factors. The wheels of business continue to spin faster but make less profit as the value of money drops. Like Alice, one runs to stay in the same place but one has to run three times faster to move forward. In all depressions, of whatever kind, the basic investment strategy is similar. First, your money should be in a strong currency (preferably several), and the chances are that if your country is going into a depression your currency is not strong. Secondly, you should be reasonably liquid, for these days when one country sneezes most others sooner or later catch cold too, and so you have to be fairly fast at moving money from one currency to another. This requires liquidity. If you are really brave, then of course there is much money to be made on the short side. Stocks move down much faster and more dramatically than they move up, but this sort of investment is not for the fainthearted, for if you are wrong on timing then your position can be wiped out before the stock turns down. For more details on how to speculate and invest in depressions I suggest two of my books on this subject: *Bear Markets—How to Survive and Make Money in Them*, Prentice-Hall, 1964; and *Panics and Crashes and How You Can Make Money Out of Them*, Arlington House, 1972.

Descending Triangles

In chart formation; a triangle with a flat bottom (see diagram). A descending triangle is considered an indication that the stock will move down drastically once it breaks the formation. The theory behind the

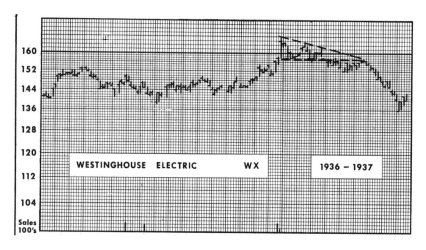

DESCENDING TRIANGLES

Chart courtesy John Magee, Inc.

formation is that possibly somebody is trying to buy a large block of stock with orders placed below the market. As these orders are hit, the market bounces off the buy points. If the rallies that such buying generates cannot be sustained (this would be shown by lower and lower rally peaks), an overhang of selling pressure and so an inherent weakness may be suspected.

Deutsche Mark

Currency of West Germany. Short form: DM. In 1948 it replaced the old Reichsmark. The DM has since then proved to be the world's strongest currency. The German government has revalued it upward in international terms four times in the last twenty-five years, an unparalleled record of strength.

Devaluation of Currency

Reduction of a currency's international value. At present the world is essentially on a U.S. dollar exchange standard; hence devaluation involves a reduction of a currency's value in terms of that dollar. What happened in 1967 to the pound sterling is an example. Until 1967 the international value of the pound sterling was set at $2.80; then it was given a new value of $2.40, a devaluation of approximately 16 percent.

The devaluation of the U.S. dollar itself involves a special process, for it is the only currency officially tied to gold. In 1934 President Roosevelt established the value of the dollar as 1/35th of an ounce of gold. In December 1971 the U.S. dollar was devalued from that ratio through a reduction of the gold content. Thereafter the value of a dollar was defined as 1/38th of an ounce of gold.

Devaluations have been a very common occurrence during the past thirty years. In fact, since World War II almost every currency on earth has been devalued. One of the exceptions is the Swiss franc. Devaluations are particularly common in Latin America, where it is not unusual for a currency to be devalued three or four or even a half a dozen times a year. The reason for devaluations is essentially always the same, namely excessive domestic inflation. A country's prices become more and more out of line with those of the rest of the world, or of its main trading partners. It becomes unattractive for foreigners to buy the goods of that country. Conversely, it becomes attractive for its citizens to buy goods in the international market, where prices are not rising as rapidly. The result is a growing deficit in the country's balance of trade as well as its balance of payments. In order to redress the dual situation and to avoid international bankruptcy, the government is then forced to reduce the international value of its currency through a process of devaluation. Except for a very brief period during 1971, the world has been essentially on a system of fixed exchange rates, with these rates between currencies being allowed to fluctuate only in a very limited fashion. This is one of the rules of the **International Monetary Fund** (see), the organization established in 1944 as the guardian of the world monetary system. A devaluation always involves a secret governmental decision, followed by an abrupt and often major change in its fixed exchange rate. Usually devaluations occur during a weekend, when the banks and stock exchanges are closed.

The private investor who fears that his currency will be devalued can best find protection in the forward foreign-exchange markets. There he is able to sell short his suspect currency against that of a hard currency. Such a type of protection is, however, usually only available in most countries to investors of substantial means and with close working relationships with major international banks. Alternatively, the smaller investors can simply send their money to a foreign bank (e.g., in Switzerland) and have their currency exchanged for a harder currency. This will not only avoid a loss but will make a profit when the hard currency is later exchanged for the newly devalued currency. (See also **Revaluation**.)

Diamond

A cousin to the **head and shoulders** (see) top formation on charts. It is a relatively rare market formation, and only in very rare cases can it occur at the *bottom* of a market. In any event it is always a reversal pattern.

Direct Taxation

Taxes levied directly on income. Personal income tax and corporation tax are forms of direct taxation. Direct taxation stands in contrast to indirect taxation, under which taxes are not levied on income but on goods and services. Purchase (sales) tax and luxury taxes are forms of indirect taxation.

Dirty Floating. See Floating

Disagio

Opposite of agio. Instead of a premium over par price, it is a discount on par price. If a security had a par value of $100 and was selling for $90, it would be at a disagio of 10 percent.

Diversification

Spreading of investments and therefore of risks. When applied to a private investor, it means that in his investment portfolio he would spread his holdings among perhaps ten or twenty different types of securities, and also in companies involved in different types of industries. When applied to a corporation, diversification usually refers to its efforts to spread its activities to new fields of endeavor. For example, an electronics firm might decide to enter the retail field in order to widen its range of activities. Diversification is justified on the grounds that there are no sure things in investment. One can't be certain of any single area. Risk-spreading insures that if one area goes sour one may still be doing well in another. To put all your eggs in one basket and then watch the basket may seem clever in theory, but in practice it is both difficult and too much of a gamble for the prudent investor. One should, however, guard against *over*diversification. Having a hundred stocks, for example, is ridiculous; for no one can adequately monitor that many different situations daily. A suitably diversified mix might be to divide your assets among good-quality blue-chip stocks, real estate, overseas investments, foreign stocks, gold coins, mining interests (either stocks or actual part ownership in mines), and possibly a small fund for quick in-and-out speculative ventures. The main object of the exercise is to keep assets in *different* fields.

Dividends

Payments made by corporations to their shareholders, normally in the form of cash. It is also possible for corporations to declare a *stock dividend*, under which shareholders receive new stock or share participation in the company instead of a cash payment.

Dollar Diplomacy

Effort on the part of the United States to influence another country through its financial power, the power of the dollar. The term has been especially used in reference to Latin America, where American big business, which had made large investments there, worked together with the United States government to exercise a certain amount of control.

Examples were found in the banana republics of Central America, which often were totally reliant on U.S. corporations for maintaining the viability of their economies. Dollar diplomacy was resented because it often implied that everyone and everything had a price tag and if the Yankee bid high enough he could have his way, regardless of the rights or wrongs of a situation. The practice is not so common anymore; but the phrase lingers on, being applied to any use of raw dollars as a substitute for good manners and consideration.

Dollar-Gold Link

For many years the value of the dollar and the value of gold were linked together. In 1934 the value of one U.S. dollar was fixed as 1/35th of an ounce of gold. Where international intergovernmental transactions were concerned, gold and dollars were freely interchangeable. It was possible for any foreign government to come to the U.S. government at any time and exchange its dollars for gold, or vice versa. The gold-dollar link was abandoned in August 1971, with the dollar ceasing to be convertible. Thereafter the U.S. government redefined the value of the dollar as being 1/38th of an ounce of gold, but it did not restore the dollar-gold link. To do so would have been almost impossible, since in the meantime the price of gold in the free markets of Western Europe had risen to almost $50 per ounce. Since then it has risen to $70. Then the U.S. again redefined the dollar's value (via a devaluation in early 1973), this time to 1/42nd of an ounce. In this period gold shot up above $90 briefly. Most economists believe that a restoration of the gold-dollar link would be possible only if the official price of gold as defined by the United States government were substantially increased, probably to $70 or $80 per ounce. In the past the gold-dollar link was an important moderator in U.S. monetary policy, for it meant that U.S. government politicians could not inflate at will; otherwise there would have been a run on gold and out of the dollar.

Dollar Premium

In the United Kingdom, the extra cost or premium that investors must pay to buy dollars for investment outside the country. Since World

War II the U.K. has had foreign exchange controls that preclude its residents from freely buying dollars for use either inside or outside the country. However, as a result of generations of foreign investments, many British individuals and corporations hold sizable dollar investments, especially in the United States. The British government allows such individuals to sell their investments and to resell the dollar proceeds to other (resident) individuals or corporations that desire to invest abroad. When they purchase such dollars, however, they must pay this premium, which has been as high as 40 percent and as low as 10 percent, depending on supply and demand at any given time.

Domicile and Residency

You are domiciled in a country if you have your roots there. You are a resident if you have obtained a residency permit, but may declare your intention to return to your country of origin some day. Generally your country of birth is your country of origin. It is also generally the country that coincides with your passport, and it is regarded as your country of domicile. Your residence is where you are actually living in some sort of semipermanent manner. The nomads and many jet-setters of this world never acquire a country of residence. Most countries will let you stay up to six months before asking you to move on or apply for residency. The stock joke of the jet set is "I can't afford to stay anywhere, I have to keep moving." This can be true. If you never acquire residency then you only pay taxes to your country of domicile, and the United States is apparently the only country that effectively taxes worldwide. So if you come from a country that does not do this, then provided you keep outside its borders (except for visits) you do not pay tax to it; and provided you move before "residency sets in," you pay no taxes anywhere else. But to the majority of people, moving every six months is too costly in personal fatigue to be a serious way of life.

This idiosyncrasy of the United States to tax its citizens no matter where they live, which many regard as a flagrant abuse of power and an unwarranted limitation on personal movement, has led to a three-tier citizen of the world—wherein such persons renounce their U.S. citizenship, acquire citizenship elsewhere (where they do not live, and thus pay no taxes), thus having three different countries: one of domicile, one of residence, one of citizenship.

Double Taxation

Many countries have what is known as a "double taxation" treaty with the United States. Unlike most older people of the world, American citizens are taxed by their government on worldwide income, no matter where they reside. If they reside and/or have their money in some foreign country, that country's government may tax their income in that country (e.g., on interest) "at source." The investor will therefore be paying tax twice. A double-taxation treaty enables the investor to claim part of the tax back, on the grounds that one set of taxation overrules the other. The advantage of a double-taxation treaty is obvious: you pay less in taxes. But the disadvantage is that if you elect to use the treaty, you violate your privacy. For many, a country with no such treaty and little or no taxation of its own is a more attractive place to live and/or place assets than one that has regular dealings and interchange of information between its own and other foreign tax authorities. It depends on what you want.

Double Tops and Bottoms

Reversal formations on stock charts. A *double top* occurs when stock prices have been trending upward, usually at high volume—prices make

DOUBLE BOTTOM

Chart courtesy John Magee, Inc.

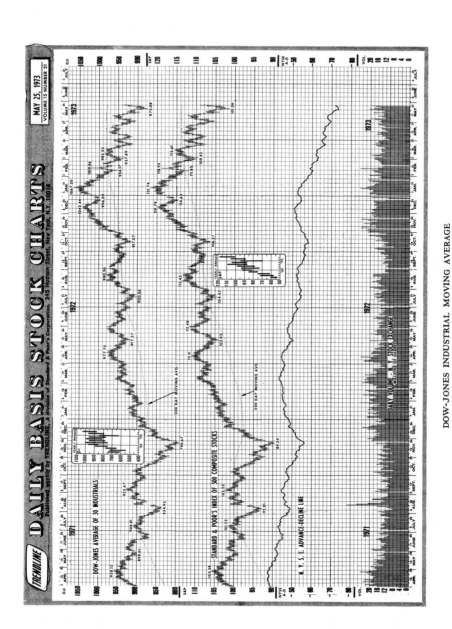

DOW-JONES INDUSTRIAL MOVING AVERAGE
DOW-JONES TRANSPORTATION MOVING AVERAGE
(The dotted lines within the price trend are the moving averages)

a new peak and then back off sharply from it, on diminishing volume, only to come back to the prior top again on slightly lower volume. From this twin peak, at least an intermediate decline is normally to be expected. A *double bottom* is exactly the same procedure in reverse, before a stock or a market turns upward.

Dow-Jones Industrial Moving Average

Index used to smooth out fluctuations in trend in hopes of giving a longer-term picture. It is calculated, like all moving averages, on the last X weeks' prices added together and the resultant figure plotted. For this particular index the Friday close for the last thirty weeks appears to be most practical to use.

Downturn

Downward movement following the peak in the business cycle. When a boom ends, an economy enters a period of downturn.

Dow Theory

Basic Dow Theory says that if the Dow-Jones Industrial average moves to a new rally high (or low), the Dow-Jones Rail Average (now the Transport Index) must do the same, thus confirming the move. The theory is that, as the two indexes represent two major areas of American investment, unless both areas move together the move is suspect and relatively localized. The theory then goes on to say that if the indexes both make a new rally high above the previous one, that is a bullish signal; if a new low, a bearish signal. Charles H. Dow (1851–1902) originally conceived his theory as an indicator of business rather than the stock market, believing that the market merely reflected what would happen in business. As both the Industrial and Transport indexes have changed drastically since Dow's day and no longer represent the same segments of the American economy that they once did, the theory has fallen in popularity. However, there are still people who put much store by its use, and indeed a couple of advisory services use it as their main indicator. It is not as simple a theory as the short definition here indicates. Books have been written to explain it. Its proper application requires considerable familiarity with its nuances. The theory is widely

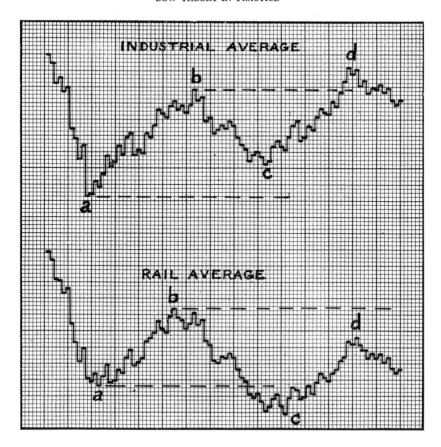

A hypothetical daily market chart to show how one average may fail to confirm
the other's Dow signal. Closing prices, indicated by short horizontal dashes, are
connected with vertical lines to make the day-to-day trend easier to follow.
Chart courtesy John Magee, Inc.

misquoted, misunderstood, and maligned, often because of insufficient
knowledge concerning it. It is probably at worst a useful backstop tool,
while at best it can be a basic guide to overall market strategy. Both
these premises assume a reasonable understanding of all its aspects.

Earned Income

Income derived directly from the efforts of an individual or corporation as a wage earner or producer. It stands in contrast to unearned in-

come, which is income that an individual or a corporation receives as a result of its investments. Usually, different rates of taxation are applied on these two types of income. The term "unearned" is slightly socialistic, since almost all money is earned. Investments of today came from money earned yesterday. If one is taxed on it first as income and then again on any fruits that come from its investment, it is punitive taxation and unenlightened, socialistic tax policy.

England. See United Kingdom

Entrepreneur

Self-starting type of businessman. Typically, an entrepreneur will start a new business based upon either a new idea or a new product and almost singlehandedly build it up into a thriving enterprise—often a major corporation. The entrepreneur is a key element in the free-enterprise system, since it is he who is responsible for the continual injection of new dynamism into the system. Entrepreneurs are the Michelangelos of capitalism.

Equipment Bond

Bond guaranteed by pledging (or mortgaging) of specific types of equipment such as railroad cars or ships.

Estate Duty

English term used to denote what in the United States is known as inheritance tax. It is a tax on property of a deceased person.

Eurodollars

U.S. dollars on deposit at banks outside the United States, usually in Europe. It is as simple as that. *Eurosterling* is sterling on deposit at banks outside the United Kingdom. Euromarks are West German marks on deposit at banks outside West Germany, and so on. Eurodollars and their counterparts in other currencies are a relatively new phenomenon. They first came into being in the early 1950s and were invented by, of all people, the Russians. It happened like this. The Soviet Union, since the Revolution, has always conducted almost all of its foreign trade in terms of U.S. dollars, since the ruble was not and still is not convertible. Even during the darkest cold-war days this practice did not change. As a result, the Soviet banking system and especially the Foreign Trade Bank and its subsidiaries in London and Paris were forced to maintain high balances of dollars as "lubrication." Under as sinful a procedure as is imaginable in banking circles, these large quantities of dollars simply lay idle, but there were good reasons. For under what everyone assumed to be an immutable law of nature, dollars were deposited, lent, or borrowed only in the United States, just as financial transactions in sterling were restricted to the United Kingdom, in rubles to the Soviet Union, and so forth. For the U.S.S.R. to have lent dollars in the United States in the early 1950s would have been less than prudent, because Russia was in debt to the States for umpteen billion dollars, for everything ranging from defaulted Czarist railroad bonds to World War II Lend-Lease. Sequestration loomed over every Soviet dollar deposited in the States. So the Communists came up with a very simple solution: lend dollars in Europe—deposit them with European banks! European banks, with their traditional lack of imagination, at first asked "But who will borrow dollars in Europe?" The answer was simple: the subsidiaries of U.S. corporations that were just starting to invade Europe. Such companies felt really "at home" only in dollars, and preferred to stick to that currency wherever they might be in the world. Thus a very important money market was born.

Today the Eurodollar market has an estimated size of around $75 billion. It is unique in that no national government has any control over it. This situation led to the creation of other Eurocurrencies, such as Eurosterling and Euro Swiss francs. The borrowing of pounds in the United Kingdom by nonresidents is severely restricted. Even in Switzerland the borrowing of Swiss francs by nonresidents in amounts exceeding ten million francs is subject to government clearance. Transactions done in these currencies outside the country could, however, not be controlled. This factor became increasingly important, for since August 15, 1971, severe limitations have been imposed on the amount of funds that nonresidents can deposit in local currencies on an interest-bearing basis in the United Kingdom, Switzerland, Germany, and many other countries. But there are no limitations—no limitations whatsoever—on

Eurocurrency placements. One other important characteristic of the Eurocurrency market must also be mentioned. It is a wholesale money market, predominantly involving only large banks and large international corporations. The typical amount dealt in is $1 million. Since private investors usually do not work with such large sums of cash, it is not easy for them to gain access to the Eurocurrency markets. You need the cooperation of a bank. Swiss banks have by far the most experience in this area, that is, in giving private investors access to this wholesale international money market.

Let us describe the procedure for getting into Eurocurrency placement step by step. We'll assume that you either want to diversify away from holding only dollars or prefer the safety of hard Eurocurrencies to that of the U.S. dollar. So Eurodollar placements are out. But you have found that Swiss banks will accept only SwFr 50,000 on an interest-bearing basis, the German banks will accept only DM 50,000, British banks only £20,000, and so on. After having taken advantage of these opportunities, you still have, say, $50,000 you would like to place abroad, on an interest-bearing basis, free of interest-equalization tax and free of any foreign taxes. So you call your Swiss bank, and ask if it would be willing to make a Eurocurrency placement for you in, say, six months Eurosterling, on a trust basis (see **Trust Account** for details). Normally the bank will agree and will tell you that the minimum amount it will accept on such a basis is $25,000. Smaller banks will go as low as $10,000.

European Economic Community (EEC); Common Market

Synonymous terms designating a group of European countries joined in an economic union. The basis of the union was the Treaty of Rome, signed in 1957. There were six original members: France, West Germany, Italy, Belgium, the Netherlands, and Luxembourg. The first stage in the development of total union was the establishment of a customs union among the six. All trade barriers and quotas were progressively eliminated so that there is now essentially free trade among the Six in the same fashion as there is free trade among the states of Iowa, Nebraska, and Pennsylvania. The objectives of the EEC go much beyond this, however. What is foreseen is the total economic integration of the economies of these countries in all trade, financial, and even monetary areas. Thus it is foreseen that after some years of further development the Common Market will end up with a common currency. The EEC is in the process of steady growth. The United Kingdom, Denmark, and Ireland became full members at the end of 1972. The EEC sphere of influence also extends beyond Western Europe. Many countries of Africa, former colonies of France or of the United Kingdom, have become associated with the EEC and have special trading privileges as a result. The EEC is today, as an economic bloc, the third most powerful unit in the world, following the United States and the Soviet Union. There can be no doubt that the EEC and its members will be one of the most potent economic factors to be reckoned with in the latter part of the twentieth century. (See also **Brussels.**)

European Free Trade Association (EFTA)

Economic grouping of countries set up in 1960 as a counterbalance to the European Common Market or European Economic Community. It embraced seven nations: The United Kingdom, Switzerland, Sweden, Norway, Denmark, Portugal, and Ireland. The founders of the European Free Trade Association had objectives quite different from those of the founders of the European Common Market. Technically both wanted, at least in the initial stages, to establish free trade among the member countries and erected a *common* external tariff vis-à-vis the rest of the world. But the European Free Trade Association, which also established free trade among member nations, decided that its member nations should retain *individual* tariff barriers vis-à-vis the rest of the world. In other words, there was no communization of the trade barriers, including tariffs and other measures, among the member nations of this grouping. The long-term aspiration of the European Free Trade Association at its founding was not to survive as an abiding entity but rather to find ways and means for its members to join the Common Market, either as direct members or associates. This objective came to partial fruition in the early 1970s when three of its members, Britain, Ireland, and Denmark, qualified for full membership in the European Common Market. The European Free Trade Association will probably disappear within a few years.

Exchange

Place or organization that regularly conducts the buying and selling of items of value, though the items themselves are not necessarily shown in the place where the trade takes place. The function of an exchange normally also extends to the supervision of the transfer and payment involved in such trade. "Exchange" is often also employed to denote the building in which such trade takes place. There are a wide variety of exchanges. The best known are stock exchanges, commodity exchanges, and foreign-currency exchanges. Exchanges had their origin in Europe in the thirteenth and fourteenth centuries, especially in the major commercial centers of Holland. The exchanges at that time were considerably different in their working from those of today. At first they amounted to nothing other than quite informal but regular get-togethers of traders and commercial people to exchange important trading and commercial information, to establish commercial relations, and to conclude trading operations. Normally, however, during those very early years the contracts were not executed in the exchange proper but were concluded outside the exchange under the supervision of a notary. In the year 1531 the government of the city of Antwerp established a special building for such purposes, and therefore Antwerp is considered the first place in the world to formally establish an exchange.

In 1608 another exchange was founded, in Amsterdam, and it was especially under the influence of the foreign trading companies domiciled in the Netherlands such as the Netherlands East Indies Company (founded in 1602) and the West Indies Company (founded in 1622). As a result of the establishment of this exchange and the activities of these two corporations, the Amsterdam exchange developed into the most important exchange of the seventeenth century. Already at that time transactions in securities—even forward transactions—were being handled in the Amsterdam exchange. But in the sixteenth century, exchanges had been founded in other places. In London an exchange was established in 1566 by Thomas Gresham (father of the famous Gresham's law), but this exchange was more or less restricted to traffic in bills of exchange. Another institution, called the Royal Exchange, was predominantly involved in trading in different types of money. It is, however, from the original English activity of trading in bills of exchange that the word "exchange" has been derived.

The word used in continental Europe for exchange is "*bourse*," a French term; "*Börse*" is the spelling in German. Today the most important security exchanges in the world are in New York, London, Frankfurt, Tokyo, Zurich, Paris, and Amsterdam, and probably in that order of importance. The two big centers for commodity exchanges are Chicago and London. Exchanges dealing in foreign currencies are centered in Frankfurt and Paris.

Exchange Controls

Measures introduced by governments to prevent their citizens from freely exchanging the currency of their country for currencies of other countries. Under typical foreign-exchange controls, it is necessary for a citizen to make an application to his government when he wants to buy the currency of another country and give that government good reason why he should be allowed to do so. Normally such purchases are not allowed for anything other than business investments abroad which his government feels in the long run will bring more foreign exchange into the country than the original outflow of its own currency. Countries having some foreign-exchange controls are the rule rather than the exception. Indeed, only a handful have none at all. The excuse given for introducing any form of exchange controls is usually related to the country's running balance-of-payments deficits. Such deficits arise because the price levels in the country no longer allow it to be competitive in world markets and thus more money flows out than comes in. Foreign-exchange controls are artificial methods, artificial barriers. They may hide but do not correct the fundamental disequilibrium in which these countries find themselves. Politicians turn to exchange controls rather than correcting the imbalances that caused the condition they use as reasons to invoke the draconian regulations. Exchange controls are a basic violation of the rights of a citizen. They often prevent his traveling or moving to another country. It is questionable that exchange controls achieve their purpose. Britain has had them for many years, and there is not a shred of evidence that they have saved the country a single pound, on balance; for such rules cause citizens to scheme to circumvent them, and money flows out that would otherwise stay in, just because of the fear of being trapped. Enforcement costs are vastly more than any possible minor gain. But the illusion continues, just like the illusion that government can create money without the people realizing its debasement and without causing any serious inflation. Exchange controls and inflation are tools of the politician against a citizenry.

Exchange Rates

Rates governing the purchase of one currency with another. For example, in September 1973 the rate of exchange between the Italian lira and the U.S. dollar was 565.75 lire = $1.00.

Ex-dividend

When a stock trades "ex-dividend," it means that on that day a dividend was paid on the share, and this amount is deducted from the share price; thus, automatically on the ex-dividend day the share trades lower by the amount of the dividend paid per share. Such days are normally marked on statistic sheets with the letter "X," to draw attention to the abnormality in that day's price.

Expenses

Outgoing payments or the buildup of obligations in return for receiving goods, services, etc. Expense items include a number of different types of cost, such as rent, upkeep of plant and equipment, and insurance premiums. The opposite of expense is *income*.

Exports

The sale abroad of goods and services. When an American company sells a machine to someone in France, it is regarded as an export. Likewise if an insurance company sells policies abroad, the transaction is regarded as an export. Where goods are concerned, one refers to *visible exports*. Where services are concerned, they are termed *invisible exports*.

Fan Line

A chartist's term. When a stock-market average (or an individual stock) reacts from a peak, the first few days of that reaction tend to be steep; indeed the steep decline can continue for up to about two weeks.

Then typically a minor rally occurs. When a reversal again occurs and the move continues downward, generally the decline is less precipitous. Hence already on that chart two downward trend lines are possible, the first a quite steep one and the second not so steep. The subsequent minor rallies and declines usually continue this rounding-out process, and so a series of what are known as fan lines can be drawn in to show where the upward resistance points are. Another way to describe them is simply as *trend lines,* emanating from the same starting point, as from a lady's fan. This is true both of uptrends and downtrends. The real significance of such fan lines comes to bear when there is a penetration of the third fan line. Historically this usually means, in the case of upward fan lines, that the stock (or market) will now become bearish.

Federal Reserve System

Central banking system of the United States, founded on December 23, 1913. It is comprised of twelve reserve banks, one being located in each of the twelve Federal Reserve Districts. The Federal Reserve Board controls credit and currency issuance and formulates monetary policy. It is run by a board of governors. The chairman is appointed by the President of the United States.

Fiduciary

An entity who acts on your behalf in a trust function. His duty legally is defined as acting solely in the interest of the person whom he represents. Executors and agents are fiduciaries. There is also the special role of fiduciary (see **Trust Account**) where a bank, particularly a Swiss bank, will act on your behalf to place funds in other countries for you. They merely act as agents for placement, not as portfolio managers.

Financial Times (London)

Far and away the best English-language newspaper in the world for business, economic, and financial news. Those interested in keeping abreast of such news on an international scale should subscribe, by airmail, no matter where in the world they live. Americans, for example, can get it one day or a few days late in any part of the States. Its coverage is not only broad but largely impartial, generally free from national bias. This broad coverage includes in-depth news from every country of the world, areas which often receive little or no coverage in any other newspaper anywhere outside of the originating country. The *Financial Times* also carries regular special sections on various countries. It publishes daily quotations from every stock exchange of note. It provides vast coverage and quotes on South African mines.

It is known simply as "the FT" around the globe. It is also sometimes called the pink sheet, since it is printed on a pink or coral-colored paper. The London headquarters address is Bracken House, Cannon Street, London E.C.4.

Many people, North and South Americans for example, are shocked when they first read the FT (after having had a diet of purely national papers like the *Wall Street Journal,* which covers little in depth other than U.S. news and U.S. company reports, and discover "there's a big world out there.") *It is a world that goes virtually unreported in the United States,* whose press is world-renowned for its provincialism. Perhaps the American press is not to be criticized very severely for this phenomenon, however, since it gives the mass public what it wants. The British concept is the reverse, both in radio, TV, and the press; the British seek always to *raise* the level of debate and comment, to give inspiration and guidance and to lift the intellectual standard. The BBC, for example, won't pander to the tastes of the mass man, but rather seeks to raise the mass man's tastes to a higher level. This is true perhaps in only a slightly lesser degree in most of continental Europe. The U.S. concept tends to be, via Madison Avenue: "If the average mental age of viewers or readers is 12, we'll scale everything we produce down to that level, in order to sell them more." It is a debatable premise, though it has unquestionably aided the cause of mass production.

Flags and Pennants

Chartist's terms. A flag (or pennant) formation on a chart looks almost exactly like its name. After a steep uptrend (the flagpole), a small oblong of prices sloping downwards occurs. This drooping-flag formation is a consolidation formation and will usually occur on lower volume. The movement can go on for as much as about three weeks but usually goes on only five to ten days. A flag formation normally precedes a continuation of the movement already begun (i.e., upward). It is possible to detect the movement in a similar formation on a major downmove, in which case the flag slopes upwards, and on completion of the consolidation the downmove continues. But a down flag is rarer.

FLAGS AND PENNANTS

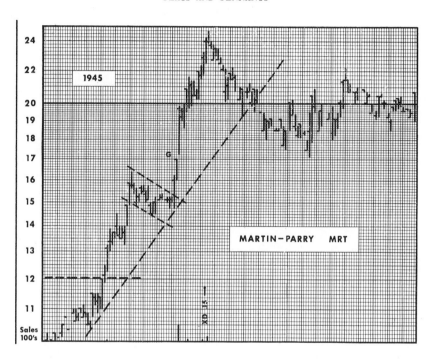

Floating

Process under which a country's currency is allowed to find its own level in foreign exchange markets. Floating represents a major exception to the recognized rules of the international monetary system as laid down in the statutes of the International Monetary Fund, founded in 1944 as a world guardian of the monetary system. Those nations who are members of the International Monetary Fund agreed that they would maintain the rates of exchange of their currencies at fixed rates, relative to the United States dollar as well as to other currencies. Thus, normally, only minimal fluctuations around the so-called parity of currency are allowed. In order to contain any fluctuation in the value of their currency, IMF members are obligated to intervene when the price of their currencies varies too greatly from this central fixed point, called the *parity*. When floating is introduced, all such intervention is abandoned, and the currency is allowed to fluctuate freely, subject only to market forces. The IMF frowns on floating. A number of countries have allowed their currencies to float for limited periods of time, especially in part of 1971–73. Included in this floating process were the German mark, the Canadian dollar, the South African rand, the British pound, and the Japanese yen. The prevalence of what is called *dirty floating* means that in practice very few countries really let their currency go. They quietly intervene on exchange markets, i.e., support or restrain their currency if it starts to move too far (in their opinion) up or down. So free market forces are not fully in effect in these cases, which regrettably are a majority of floats. There are of course degrees of dirtiness, i.e., of government intervention. Politicians seldom practice what they preach about free enterprise and free markets or indeed freedom of any kind.

Foreign Exchange

Dealings in currencies of different nations. The foreign-exchange market is generally divided into two areas: the *spot* market, where currencies in cash form change hands on the spot, and the *forward* market, where currencies are bought and sold for delivery at some time in the future (generally between one month and one year).

Frankfurter Allgemeine

West Germany's leading newspaper, published in Frankfurt am Main. It is like the *Neue Zürcher Zeitung* in Switzerland, a liberal (in the European meaning) newspaper, dedicated to the concept of free enterprise. The sophisticated international investor will subscribe to this newspaper along with the *Neue Zürcher Zeitung* (if he can read German) and the *Financial Times* if he intends to follow international investment, financial, and monetary events.

Fundamentals

Over the years in Wall Street there have developed two distinct schools of thought on the best way to predict future stock action. One school, which believes that all can be seen in the *movement* of the stock and nothing else, are "technicians," and those who believe in looking behind the stock are "fundamentalists." Fundamentals are the bust, waist, and hip measurement—the vital statistics of a stock, such as its annual report, how the company is run, what sort of dividend it pays, whether the product has a good future, how much is going into research, what management is like, past and projected earnings. The problem with studying only the fundamentals of a stock is that it is almost impossible to know all there is to know about a company. Somebody, somewhere, will know more, if only the chairman of the board. Also, government action on an economic level can precipitate a move in ALL stocks that cannot be predicted by reading company reports. By *also* watching the movement of a stock on a chart and attempting to assess patterns in its movement, it is often possible to see action in a stock which shows that somebody knows something that perhaps you don't know. Hence for the best market analysis, fundamentals, technical considerations, and political and politico-economic considerations should all be assessed.

Funding Bonds. See **Participation Bonds**

Futures, Commodity. See **Commodity**

Futures, Currency. See **Currency Futures**

German Central Bank. See **Bundesbank**

Gibraltar

A tax haven. Gibraltar is a self-governing British colony at the southern tip of Spain. Income tax for residents rises progressively to a maximum of 30 percent. Tax-exempt companies can be set up in Gibraltar for firms not doing any business in the precincts of the island. Also, companies that do business only with other tax-exempt companies on "the Rock" fall into the "external company" status. Taxation of resident companies is a flat 40 percent. Generally Gibraltar welcomes people wishing to retire there. You must show at least $5,000 for each married couple as an initial qualification. A work permit is very difficult to obtain.

Gilt-Edged

Term applied in Anglo-Saxon countries to high-quality or first-class securities, especially bonds. So called gilt-edged securities are normally those issued by governments or by extremely large and solid corporations. In the United Kingdom the term is reserved strictly for government securities.

Giro. See Postal Checking Systems

Gnomes of Zurich

Term coined by George Brown when he was the Labour Chancellor of the Exchequer to describe the people in the banking community of Zurich involved in foreign-exchange speculation. Foreign exchange has always been a specialty of Swiss banks. It is they or people who use their facilities who sell currencies short when they consider them to be devaluation candidates. One of their prime targets during the 1960s was the pound sterling, since it was a soft currency that experienced recurrent difficulties. The term is of course derogatory, implying that these are evil little men who take advantage of a country's economic difficulties for selfish ends. The term is most unfair since shorting of currency is usually done by speculators, not Swiss bankers. Such selling may well be done through Swiss banks, but it is done in the main on behalf of clients. But the Swiss are accustomed to being blamed for the activities of their customers. And not everyone regards the gnomes as evil. Some see them as friendly little elves who are trustworthy custodians of their money, silent and loyal and obedient. It probably depends on whether you are an IRS agent or a Swiss bank depositor. The historian T. R. Fehrenbach commented on the gnome reference, "What really infuriated Mr. Brown and Labour MP's was that the men they disparaged as gnomes were really giants."

Going Public

A phrase denoting that a previously privately owned firm will be
listing itself on a stock exchange (or over-the-counter market) and
selling its shares to the public at large. Going public gives a firm publicity,
wider distribution of its stock (and thus presumably more people with
a vested interest in seeing the company prosper), a chance to raise new
money via stock issues that are interest-free, etc. There are drawbacks
as well; for example, it is expensive. The decision usually hinges on the
size of the company. See also **Public Corporation (or Company).**

Gold Exchange Standard

This is really a dollar standard by another name, as it existed up to
July 1971. Under this system the dollar served as an international reserve currency under the condition that dollars were freely convertible
into gold, i.e., could be exchanged into gold, upon demand on the U.S.
Treasury by a foreign government. The vice versa of course also applied:
gold could be delivered to the U.S. Treasury in exchange for dollars
at a fixed price ($35 an ounce) at any time. With the suspension
of gold/dollar convertibility the gold exchange standard came to an
end.

Gold Fixing

The gold bullion price is established twice daily in Zurich, Paris, and
London. In these three financial centers at around 10:30 each morning
and 3:30 each afternoon, brokers or banks that specialize in the trading
of gold bullion get together and establish a price for the metal among
themselves. If the buy orders in the market exceed the sell orders, at
this group meeting they will mark up the gold price. Of course, when
the opposite is true it will be dropped. This does not mean that the
price fixed in this session is valid throughout the day. After the
fixing there is an after market where gold may well exchange hands
between buyers and sellers at a price varying somewhat, though not
considerably, from the fixing arranged earlier.

Gold Hoarding

Process under which individuals convert their money into gold bullion and store it indefinitely. The reason for gold hoarding, which is very prevalent in such countries as France, Switzerland, and India, is that gold is regarded by many individuals as the ultimate store of value. This view is natural for people in countries with high rates of inflation who have seen their currencies devalued time after time while gold maintained its value, especially its international value. Gold hoarding continues to represent a major factor in the international gold markets: it is estimated that often between 10 and 20 percent of total new gold output disappears into private gold hoards. It is also estimated that around 50 percent of the world's gold is in private hands. The word "hoarding" has a somewhat negative ring, implying that gold holders are miserly and even sinister. It is a term coined by politicians to try to shame people out of defending their assets and to get them instead to line up, sheeplike, for whatever slaughter the government has in mind for the national currency (debasing it via inflation, by withdrawing its backing, by making it inconvertible, etc.). But the so-called gold hoarder is simply trying to defend himself against politicians who are watering down the national currency. Indeed, *not* to hoard is seen by some as the attitude of one who doesn't care about his family's future or the eventual value of his savings. Casting gold savers in the role of evil "hoarders" paves the way for politicians to legislate that citizens cannot legally hold gold, as has happened in many countries.

Gold Standard

A monetary system developed (by evolving, not by plan) in the nineteenth century under which the supply of money in circulation in a country was determined by the amount of gold reserves. It was self-regulating. If gold reserves went up, the amount of money in circulation would increase automatically. This in turn would create domestic inflation. As a result the country's international trade position would deteriorate, leading to a situation where the balance of payments would go into deficit. This would lead to an outflow of gold, a reduction of money in circulation resulting in a process of deflation, which in turn would bring the country's international payments position back into equilibrium.

This system was essentially abandoned in 1933. It provided one hundred years of stable prices and prosperity in Great Britain and some other countries.

Good Till Canceled (G.T.C.). See **Buy Orders and Sell Orders**

Graph Paper. See **Arithmetical Graph Paper**

Gresham's Law

Gresham's law states that if there are two different types of money in circulation, the "bad money" (the weaker) eventually drives out the good. This law was formulated by the Englishman Thomas Gresham (1519–79), who as a result of the study of money patterns and systems reached the conclusion that this "law" is one with historical validity. The good money is withdrawn from circulation and is hoarded for its intrinsic value. "Let's keep the good stuff and spend the other" is the *modus vivendi*.

Gross National Product (GNP)

Total output of a country—all goods and services—as expressed in monetary terms. In recent decades the gross national product statistics have come to be regarded as the prime measure of a country's economic performance. One must, however, use this statistical measure with great care, for it does not reflect the effects of inflation—the GNP of a country can increase by 10 percent merely because the *prices* of the goods and services increased by 10 percent, with no real growth in total output. When employing GNP as a measure, it is best to deflate it by employing the GNP price index so that one can for example compare the total output of a country in 1963 with that in 1973 at *constant* prices. The result is what is termed *real* GNP growth, a more nearly true measure of the increases in output which a national economy achieves during a given period of time.

Many serious analysts question the manner in which the U.S. GNP is calculated; they claim that it is distorted, with a bias in favor of constant growth. Even some *debt* makes the GNP rise, whereas perhaps it should be deducted. Furthermore, the government's method of computing inflation rates is widely believed to be outdated and to understate true inflation by approximately 3 percent a year. This is said to be because it is based more on goods than on services, though the United States has become a service-oriented country—and the cost of services has gone up much more sharply than the cost of goods. There is obviously a need for some serious research into a true measuring system, both for GNP and for inflation. The present method serves the interests of politicians, for it helps foster the appearance of growth and plays down inflationary effects. To get government to accept a more accurate method seems unlikely. Meanwhile each of us must be his own economist.

Group of Ten

An unofficial grouping of the most prosperous nations of the world, which coordinate their policies in the international monetary sphere. The members are: the United States, Canada, Britain, Japan, West Germany, France, Belgium, the Netherlands, Italy, and Sweden. Switzerland is an unofficial eleventh member. It was the Group of Ten that in 1971 arranged the realignment of all major currencies, including the official devaluation of the dollar in December of that year. At the Bretton Woods conference in 1944 it was intended that the International Monetary Fund would act as the guardian of the world monetary system and provide the forum in which the nations of the world would work out their mutual currency problems. However, the International Monetary Fund, having as it does 118 members, has not been able successfully to do the job, simply because it has been too unwieldy. Therefore in the 1950s the leading (or perhaps one should say the most prosperous) nations banded together into this smaller club, the Group of Ten. They have met on an irregular basis, usually when some crisis in the international monetary sphere develops. In 1972 the IMF agreed, under pressure from the United States and certain underdeveloped nations, to expand the Group of Ten into the Group of Twenty. Whether the Ten will actually disappear as a cohesive unit is yet to be seen. Even if they do not meet separately, they will certainly dominate the Group of Twenty. The new grouping could force more decisions to be taken by the BIS (Bank for International Settlements), which is composed more or less of members of the Group of Ten. Economic power cannot be denied, however the window dressing is arranged.

Group of Twenty. See **Group of Ten**

Growth Rate

Rate of increase as expressed in percentage. If your income goes from $10,000 a year to $11,000 the next year, you have experienced a 10 percent growth rate in your income. To be realistic and not delude oneself, one must differentiate between nominal and real growth rates. Inflation can grossly distort the meaning of growth rates. If your income did increase by $1,000 in a given year but prices had increased by 6 percent, the real growth rate in your income was only 4 percent. The term "growth rate" is commonly applied more to companies or a national economy than to an individual. In recent decades growth has been almost a god, always on the assumption that growth is good, without question. Now, however, a few people are questioning this premise: Who said growth is good? Good for whom? What does growth cost? What's wrong with staying level or even dropping back? Some venture to predict growth will go out of fashion and be thought of as undesirable. It already is among many ecologists.

Hard Currency

One backed by substantial international reserves. Such reserves are usually in the form of gold and convertible currencies. But the hardness of the currency is also affected by the status of a country's balance of payments and balance of trade. A country that regularly and consistently has surpluses in its international payments is normally regarded as having a hard currency. Those countries with consistent deficits, which in time result in diminishing their gold and/or convertible currency reserves, are regarded as having soft currencies. A currency will also be thought to be becoming soft if the nation's inflation rate is rising rapidly.

Hard Money

Some of what was said about hard currency, above, holds true here, but economists are apt to think of the term "hard money" as meaning more specifically that it is backed by a high percentage of gold, as in the case of the Swiss franc. This is not a precise definition because there are mitigating factors. Nor is the term used in banking. It is more a philosophical concept. Truly conservative economists believe in "hard money," by which they generally mean a money that is convertible on demand into gold and/or silver. By this definition there is no such money in the world of today, but there was earlier in this century, and indeed for much of man's history. True conservatives long for a return to hard money, and more than one group (mainly disillusioned Americans) are at work to found a new nation that will be founded on pure laissez-faire and hard money (see **Minerva**). It is a socialist concept that money should be "soft"—i.e., not backed by gold or convertible into gold. The idea has been widely adopted by politicians because it enables them to manipulate national budgets more easily, leaving increased debt as they depart from office.

Head and Shoulders

A chartist's term designating a chart pattern that indicates the top of a market, usually a major top. There is a rally on heavy volume followed by a minor price recession on lesser volume. This is followed by a second rally on high volume; this rally reaches a slightly higher point than the previous one and then falls back again (on lower volume) to about the level of the last minor bottom, but in any event LOWER THAN THE LAST RALLY HIGH. The third rally occurs on much less volume than the prior two and fails to reach the height of the prior rally—which is called the "head." Then another decline sets in. The sell signal is indicated when the market breaks below the "neckline" (as shown in the chart)—which is the area of the last two lows, between the three rallies.

A *reverse* head-and-shoulders pattern can occur at *bottoms* of markets to indicate a reversal upward. The price movement is completely transposed (the pattern is turned upside down), but volume is the same. That is, there is a decline on heavy volume, a minor recovery on lesser volume, and another decline that takes the market below the prior low on volume heavier than in the prior minor advance but not so heavy as in the last decline. This is followed by a recovery on which volume may very well be heavier than on the prior advance. A third decline on lower volume then takes place before the rally starts. On the next advance, volume increases considerably and pushes the advance through the "neckline," confirming the "breakout."

Both of these patterns have a high degree of reliability. One can also

HEAD AND SHOULDERS

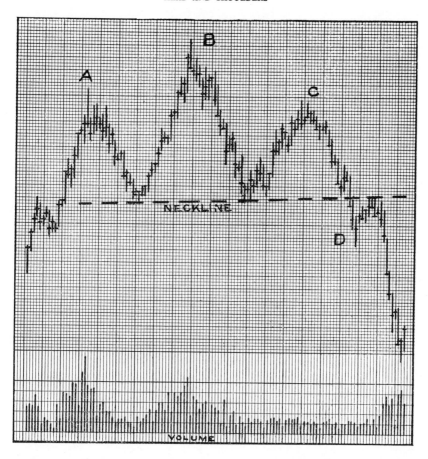

project an approximate target for the move that follows the breaking of the neckline. By measuring the distance from the top of the head to the neckline, you get the minimum number of points that usually will follow the breaking of the neckline. The minimum is often exceeded, but miraculously such moves sometimes come to a halt at precisely the measured amount indicated by the formula above. The neckline can be slanting slightly and still be valid.

Hedging

Investment technique by which one seeks to develop a program offering protection against downside risk. Hedging can take on many forms. If an investor has a large portfolio of American stocks and feels that the dollar will be devalued, he can seek to hedge against potential losses arising out of such a devaluation by selling the dollar short against a hard currency such as the German mark or Swiss franc. The term "hedge" became very popular in the securities business in New York in the 1960s, and many so called hedge funds sprang up. The philosophy of a hedge fund was not only to go long on securities but also to go short when it was felt that the market or some share was peaking out. In practice, hedge funds did not prove very successful, perhaps because the essence of success in most types of hedging ventures (especially shorting) is timing, and this demands extraordinary skill. If you short too soon or a bit late, you are achieving exactly the opposite to what you intended. It costs more to be wrong when shorting than wrong when long. Likewise, if you go short on the dollar as a hedge and the currency contract expires before devaluation, you get an equally undesirable effect.

Hedging can also be applied to less sophisticated types of investment strategy. For instance, investors who *diversify* their holdings are in essence hedging. If an investor feels that the economic outlook for his country is in general not good, he can hedge by adding foreign investments to his investment portfolio. Likewise an investor who feels that a deep recession is around the corner can hedge by accumulating a good amount of cash, and/or he may invest in those types of situation which hold up well during periods of depression, such as precious metals, the shares of gold-mining corporations, food shares, and the like. During periods of monetary uncertainty, one can hedge by having one's assets spread among several of the stronger currencies. Having all of one's capital in a single currency, whichever it is, is risky in such times—if that currency may be devalued "at some point," it is imprudent to remain heavily in it.

High-Low Index

Stock-market indicator made up of the subtraction of the daily new lows from the daily new highs, or vice versa. In order for the resulting graph line to show a general trend rather than daily fluctuation, a "moving average" is usually made. I recommend a five-day moving average, in which one subtracts the total of the last five days' lows from the total of the last five days' highs and plots the resulting figure. The index can also be made by keeping the figures for highs and lows separate. In other words, add the last five days' highs and plot this figure, and then add the last five days' lows and plot this figure as a separate line, possibly the highs in black and the lows in red. When the lines cross, look out for a major direction change.

HIGH-LOW INDEX

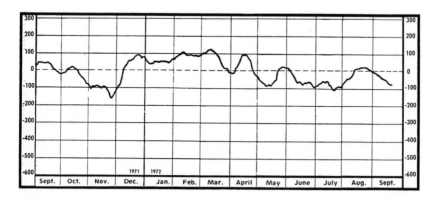

Hire Purchase

British term for consumer credit or the buying of consumer items on time payments. (Americans speak of "buying on the installment plan" or "buying on time.")

Holland. See **Amsterdam**

Hong Kong

British crown colony adjoining and off southeastern China; a tax haven. There is no tax on foreign source income. Income and profits from Hong Kong sources only are subject to tax, up to a maximum rate of 15 percent. Company profits tax: 15 percent. Property income tax: 15 percent. There is no capital gains tax, no withholding tax. Death duties: 3 percent to 25 percent. Obtaining residency is very difficult, and Hong Kong does not issue its own passports. The main interest in Hong Kong is as a possible place to set up a tax-exempt company. It is not recommended as a place to seek to live.

Immediate Orders. See **Buy Orders and Sell Orders**

Income Bond

One upon which no fixed rate of interest is paid or promised. Rather the income from the bond is a certain percentage of the profit of the issuing corporation.

Indirect Taxation. See **Direct Taxation**

Inflation

To the layman, inflation means that prices rise, and his money buys less and less. The phenomenon causes problems for everyone. Banks run low on lending power. Demands for wage increases become more frequent. For the investor who wishes to preserve his capital during inflation, the main problem is that his money will be worth less next year than this year. Money saved when prices were lower now buys less and is said to have "lost its value." There are two standard types of inflation—creeping inflation and runaway inflation. Creeping inflation is what Keynesian economists (see **Keynes, John Maynard**) say is "necessary" for prosperity. It is the 4 percent per year (or less) increase in money supply reflected in prices and cost of living, which government says it can control and which people are said to be prepared to live with. In the earlier days of the cycle it does seem to give impetus to business. The impetus probably comes from the elation one feels when one finds oneself apparently richer than one has really worked to become —the excitement of receiving an unexpected gift. But over a period of time a repetitive gift becomes commonplace and the stimulus it originally caused diminishes. The "gifts" become *necessary* to sustain the growth rate. Runaway inflation enters when government tries to strengthen the impetus by increasing the rate, which then gets out of control. Chaos is the result.

"Controlled" inflation can occur for reasons such as war, when the economy of a country is temporarily upset and over a period of a few years prices double or triple. By stringent controls and other measures (usually involving a devaluation), prices are then stabilized. Everybody is worse off by the percentage of the devaluation, but a new base is established for growth. This type of inflation is often followed by a classic depression or recession.

Economists differ violently on the *causes* of inflation but all must agree, if grudgingly in some cases, that increasing the supply of money has a direct relationship to inflation. Whether it is its *sole* cause and what the *ratio* is between upping money supply and percent of inflation, remain areas of differing opinion. But classic economists and most conservative economists tend to feel the link is very strong. They attempt to influence government to keep money pumping to as nearly nil as possible, while the so-called neo-Keynesians often favor a liberal policy of money creation in order to "encourage growth," endlessly.

Measuring inflation is another sensitive area. In the United States, for example, government yardsticks are said by many to be old-fashioned since they don't take into account the change in the U.S. economy to its present highly services-oriented status. Government price indices are heavily weighted with goods rather than services, and goods have gone up much less sharply than services. The result is a distortion, perhaps in the neighborhood of 3 percent a year; in short, U.S. inflation is perhaps being understated by 3 percentage points annually. If this criticism is valid, current figures may be preventing government from undertaking measures it would consider necessary if it were more aware of the truth. But some feel no reform of the index is likely if it suits politicians to keep an indicator that makes their management performance appear successful, or at least better than it is.

Insurance

A contract between an insurance company and an individual (or corporation) requiring coverage whereby the insurance company, for a preset fee or premium, undertakes to guarantee the insured against loss under circumstances laid out in a contract. The exact limitations of such terms are always completely defined.

Interbank Borrowing

Banks borrow money from each other for many reasons. The most important is that sometimes a bank finds itself temporarily low on liquidity and will borrow funds from other banks that have an excess of liquidity. The borrowing will often be for only a few days. Normally the interbank borrowing rates are very low. A typical mode of bank borrowing in the United States involves the use of so-called federal funds, namely, reserve funds held with the Federal Reserve System. The rate charged will be 1 to 2 percent below the prime rate.

Interest Equalization Tax

Introduced in the early 1960s by the United States government. It is a type of foreign-exchange control. Any U.S. resident who buys a foreign security must pay this special tax, which was originally 17.5 percent but was later reduced to 11.5 percent. The term "tax" was chosen because at the time of its adoption interest rates in the United States were appreciably lower than those in most other countries in the world. This made it attractive for foreign entities to borrow money in New York. But a result was an increasing outflow of funds from the American capital market, which was damaging to the U.S. balance of payments. Later, interest rates in the United States rose to and even well above those prevailing in many other countries of the world. At that point it became clear that the interest equalization tax was nothing but a type of foreign-exchange control.

The interest equalization tax is applied only to indirect investments abroad, that is, to the individual purchase of securities issued by foreign corporations. It does not apply to direct investments, that is, to the direct placement of money into foreign business or to actually starting a business abroad. Thus if an American corporation decides to acquire or associate itself with a foreign corporation through the purchase of a large block or the entire equity of that corporation, such transaction is not subject to interest equalization tax. However, for investments exceeding $100,000 the American company must receive permission from the United States Department of Commerce. Interest equalization tax is an unusually unpopular tax, perhaps because it involves red tape and places restrictions on Americans where there were none before. Other nations dislike it since it is nothing more than a tariff wall. It was intended to force Americans to buy only U.S. stocks. Like most restrictive laws, it backfired and caused a greater interest in foreign shares than ever. Nixon recognized its unpopularity by cutting the tax by more than a third. It is hoped the tax will be eliminated, since it is counterproductive.

International Bank for Reconstruction and Development

Like its sister institution the International Monetary Fund, the International Bank for Reconstruction and Development was founded at Bretton Woods in 1944. It's a mouthful to say the International Bank for Reconstruction and Development, so most call it simply the World Bank. It has the function of providing finance to the developing countries. In contrast to the aid programs of the United States and other countries, the World Bank does not give away money but provides low-interest *loans* to developing countries for specific projects. These loans are usually repayable after fifteen or twenty years. The funds of the World Bank come from the direct subscriptions of its member governments (which include most members of the United Nations) and from the issuance of bonds in many capital markets throughout the world. One interesting aspect of World Bank bonds is that even though they may be issued in Frankfurt or Zurich and denominated in German marks or Swiss francs, they are not subject to the American Interest Equalization Tax. Hence it is America and the American taxpayer which directly or indirectly supply by far the greatest amount of funds to the World Bank. The president and chief executive officer of the World Bank has always been an American.

In some people's minds there is a question whether the World Bank is a truly viable banking institution in the original sense, for as time goes by it appears increasingly unlikely that the countries to which the World Bank has extended its loans will be in a position to repay. Some seem also to have no desire to do so. Lord Keynes, one of the founding fathers of Bretton Woods, noted that the two institutions born at that conference were misnamed: that the International Monetary Fund was a bank and that the International Bank for Reconstruction and Development was really nothing more than a fund. The original purpose of the World Bank was to finance reconstruction of the world after the devastation of World War II. But after a very short time, especially when the Marshall Plan assumed most of this function, the World Bank turned to the developing (i.e., undeveloped) countries as its main objective and has taken that direction ever since. Critics of the World Bank point to the poor quality of its loans, to the arrears of interest payments, to the fact the bank survives bankruptcy only by continuing to float new bond issues. Were this a private bank, no one would invest in its bonds. Only the fact that it is subsidized by charitable donations from assorted nations gives investors confidence to buy its bonds. But some consider it risky, since the chief donor is the United States; if the U.S. ever decides to cut back its donations, the World Bank could collapse. The IMF would not necessarily fall with it because it has its own separate funds.

International Investment Letter Association (I.I.L.A.)

Organization begun in 1970 for publishers of financial advisory letters. The founder and first president was Dr. Harry D. Schultz, who was reelected in 1971. It is the only worldwide organization ever attempted for investment letters. It accepts for members only those letters which are well established and are written by their publishers (rather than produced by a vast corporation staff)—in other words, its field is the *personal* news letter. I.I.L.A. seeks to set a high standard for the field and to police its own industry, for the benefit of the public at large. Most members are from the United States, Canada, continental Europe, Great Britain, and South Africa. Information on I.I.L.A. can be obtained by writing the president at 170 Sloane Street, London, S.W.1, England.

International Monetary Fund (IMF)

The International Monetary Fund was established at the conference held in Bretton Woods, New Hampshire, in 1944. The purpose of the IMF is to serve as the guardian of the world monetary system. Currently it has 119 members. Although the bylaws and organization of the IMF are rather complex, essentially its prime function is to establish rates of exchange for the world's currencies. It is the obligation of the member countries to register their rate of exchange, in terms of U.S. dollars, with the IMF and to maintain this rate. Thus the IMF is the prime component of the system of the dollar exchange standard and of the system of worldwide fixed exchange rates. The IMF has funds of its own, contributed by member nations, which it can lend to countries to help them overcome temporary balance of payments difficulties. In addition, in the late 1960s the IMF itself began to issue a new type of reserve unit, Special Drawing Rights (SDRs). These were at that time given the name "paper gold" in that they were accounting units defined in terms of gold that could be used to settle debts between nations on the same basis as gold. The IMF has proved unwieldy because of the great number of nations involved, and the Group of Twenty (see **Group of Ten**) has taken over the prime function of implementing change in the international monetary system.

Investment Letters. See **Advisory Services** and **International Investment Letter Association**

Invisible Trade Balance

The imports and exports of a country are divided into two categories: goods and services. The import and export of services and the resulting trade balance have been described as *invisible*, obviously because physical goods are not involved but rather "invisible" services. Such invisible exports and imports play an increasingly important role in world commerce because of the spread of international banking, the worldwide nature of the insurance business, and the provision of many other types of advisory services relating to engineering projects and the like. For many countries, especially the United Kingdom and Switzerland, invisible transactions play a very important role, as these are countries which almost always have deficits in their visible trade; that is, they import more goods than they export on a consistent basis. It is through their surplus of exports over imports in the invisible field that they balance their trade with the rest of the world or achieve surpluses. The tourist business is also classed as invisible.

Ireland

A tax/citizenship haven. Ireland is a very flexible place to develop business, resident, or citizenship status (particularly if your parents or grandparents were Irish). Income tax is levied on worldwide income, if you are resident in Ireland, at the rate of 35 percent, with a surtax of 45 percent on income over $16,000. The corporate tax ranges from 7.5 percent to 23 percent, and estate (death) duties are graduated from zero to 16 percent on $75,000 to a maximum of 40 percent on estates over $250,000. If you are an artist, writer, or composer, or indeed make your living from anything that can be called "of cultural merit," your earnings are tax-free. Work permits are difficult to obtain in Ireland but residency isn't. Write: Department of Justice, 72 St. Stephen's Green, Dublin 2. Citizenship is easy if you have the proper Irish heritage; and if you set up any sort of light manufacturing business or farming, it may speed the process a bit. The tax-haven aspect of Ireland takes full effect if you operate a business from the tiny Shannon Free Airport Zone: you get a total tax holiday there for eighteen years. But it must be a real business, not a brass plate as in the Bahamas. Minimum floor space is prescribed if you operate only an office. A bonus in Ireland is that the natives are truly friendly, especially to Americans.

Isle of Man

A small island in the Irish Sea, part of the United Kingdom, a tax haven. It has a total area of 227 square miles and a population of 51,000. It is not the sort of place that one would want to live in generally. It is in many ways like the Channel Islands but with a less desirable climate. Income tax is about 23 percent on worldwide income for residents. Bank interest is tax-free. It is possible to set up a type of "exempted company" whereby if the company is controlled from abroad, no tax is payable. There is no capital-gains tax, or wealth tax, withholding tax, or death duty.

Japan

The business miracle country. The land of the rising sun becomes more American every day with its crowds, its concrete jungles, and its steel efficiency, but nonetheless it is still a very "cut-off" country, one that does not welcome the foreigner easily, either as a resident or as a fellow trader. It is virtually impossible to obtain permanent residency in Japan unless you have some special reason for being there. Japanese taxation, like all things oriental, appears complicated to the Westerner. The best way to learn about the system is to obtain *Guide to Japanese Taxes* by Taizo Hayashi, from Zaikei Shoho Sha, 1–2–13, Higashi Shimbashi, Minato-ku, Tokyo. Price ¥1,600 (that's about $6). But the tax system offers nothing by way of nonresident company set-ups that can be useful. The dramatic rise in prosperity in Japan over the past few years has been almost impossible for the foreigner to cash in on.

Even to buy Japanese shares on the Tokyo exchange is a Herculean task. However, recently Japanese brokerage houses have opened branches in the United States, specifically Nippon Securities and Nomura Securities. The easiest way for Americans to participate in the Japanese market is to buy Japan Fund, which is listed on the big board. Though it is specifically a Japanese portfolio, it has all the simplicity of handling of any American stock. There are several Swiss-bank-owned Japanese funds now also. For information on Japanese stocks I suggest you obtain *Investment in Japanese Stocks* by Nomura Securities, Ltd., from the Institute of International Investment, 2 Kudan 3-chome, Chiyodaku, Tokyo, Japan.

Johannesburg Stock Exchange Monthly Bulletin

Monthly publication on South African shares, which includes share capital, monthly volume highs, lows, rights issues, etc. It is 7.50 rand per year plus R14.40 if you want it air mail. (The rand is about $1.43.) Obtainable from Public Relations Department, Johannesburg Stock Exchange, P.O. 1174, Johannesburg, South Africa.

Kaffirs

The terms "Kaffirs" and "Kaffir market" are used by the European investment community for South African mining shares and the market dealing with them. The word "Kaffir" comes from the Arabic word meaning "infidel," and was a name given to all Africans who were not Moslems. The British and other Europeans restricted the term to the Bantu races. The word was apparently applied to the mines because so many Bantus were employed in them. But the South Africans themselves tend to avoid using the term. It is heard today mainly in Europe.

Karat

Measurement of gold content in an alloy. One karat means that 1/24th of the alloy is pure gold. The 100 percent pure metal is much too soft to be used alone, and so other metals are mixed with it to make it more serviceable. Hence 22-karat gold, which is the finest used in the manufacture of jewelry, is about 92 percent gold and the rest alloy. The gold that is used by nations to back their currency is generally in bars of .995 to .999 fineness. Karat is also the unit of weight for precious stones.

Keynes, John Maynard

British economist who is generally credited with being the father of the belief in deficit spending and cheap money to create full employment. Until the 1930s he was regarded as an orthodox economist, but during that decade, in seeking to analyze the causes of the world depression, he attacked the earlier orthodox economics and tried to show that it would be overcome only if governments deliberately encouraged investment by making loans easy. His book *The General Theory of Employment, Interest and Money* (1936) preceded by a two-volume *Treatise on Money* (1930), had a profound effect on American thought. Prior to the U.S. election of 1932, Keynes had outlined his ideas to F. D. Roosevelt and contributed greatly to formulation of the New Deal policies. His ideas also helped shape World War II finance policies in Britain. He was the chief British representative at Bretton Woods in 1944, where plans for the International Monetary Fund were formulated. So-called liberals in the U.S. are full of praise for Keynes's deficit theories, while most U.S. conservatives damn him for them. Certainly his influence has been profound over the past forty years. If the massive debts incurred by the United States in this period while following his precepts lead to an economic smash on the lines of 1929–33, then Keynesianism will be dishonored. Until such an event, the debates will continue to rage on the merits of unending debt. Professor Friedrich A. von Hayek, who was at the university with Keynes and knew him well, says Keynes renounced his deficit-spending theories before his death in 1946. The world may come to renounce them too, given time.

KontoKurrent Account. See Contocurrent Account

Laissez-Faire

The doctrine that the only duties governments should be able to perform are the keeping of the peace and the protection of property, and that all else is the right and responsibility of the individual. The arguments in favor of it are that freedom enables the individual to expand mentally, physically, and economically and that the overall prosperity and well-being of a country therefore progress most rapidly when total laissez-faire exists. The exponents of this doctrine point to the early days of American capitalism and show how a country under laissez-faire of sorts was turned from a wilderness to the major power on earth in a space of about a hundred years. The opponents argue that in major depressions (under laissez-faire) people would possibly be allowed to starve in the streets—that it would literally be a case of the survival of the fittest. In practice, laissez-faire, like communism, capitalism, or democracy, is an ideal to theorize and speculate about; as with the other "ideal" concepts, there has never been a period in the history of man when *any* of these ideologies was tried in a pure form. All societies have used some ideology as a general basis but, while arguing vehemently in favor of the concept, have never lived up to it, but rather with a compromise of it.

Land. See **Real Estate**

Laws, Antitrust. See **Antitrust Laws**

Letter of Credit

Not a credit as such but a document that provides a potential credit to either a person or a corporation or another bank. A letter of credit does not involve an immediate payment of any money at the time of issuance to the person in whose favor it has been issued. Rather it serves as a promise to pay a sum of money as specified in this letter of credit to the person to whom it is issued, should he ever demand it. The letter of credit often serves as a guarantee rather than the actual basis for a credit itself. Used this way, it enables men who don't know each other well to do business, for the letter of credit is saying, in effect: "Look, this fellow is good for $150,000, and our bank so guarantees it." It eliminates the need for businessmen to have to take each other's word about their means—they do not have to back up what they say on a given business deal. Travelers sometimes carry letters of credit if they feel they may need a substantial sum while abroad. It enables them to walk into a foreign bank and pick up cash up to the amount specified in the letter of credit.

Leverage

In the financial sense, making a given amount of money do more work than apparently is normal for its size, in exactly the same way that a lever applied scientifically can lift a very heavy weight. The power of leverage shows itself in the commodity market, where you can trade on a relatively small margin, e.g., 10 percent. **Puts and calls** (see) are a leveraged way of participating in the stock market. However, while one stands to gain more, leveraged positions are also more vulnerable if you are wrong. Leveraging is a highly speculative way of investing. It is not to be recommended for a *major* portion of assets.

Liability

A term with many meanings. In corporation accounting it is used for claims against a corporation. Liabilities can be money owed to a bank, to bondholders, or to suppliers. Also, the share capital and reserves of a corporation are listed vis-à-vis the company. On any balance sheet the assets and liabilities must by definition always be equal to each other.

Liberal

This word is a cause for great confusion among investors round the world. In the United States (and nations in the U.S. orbit) the word tends these days to mean left-of-center thinking. "Liberal" is, in fact, a dirty word among U.S. conservatives. But it wasn't always so. It used to have the meaning it still does in Europe, where it designates those who believe in free enterprise, in free marketing procedure, a conservative view of economic matters. At international economic conferences, speakers are forever having to qualify the word when they use it; they invariably add "in the European sense, that is."

Liechtenstein

A small tax-haven principality bordering on Switzerland and Austria has become famous in the world of finance because of the special tax deals it makes available to the special types of corporations known locally as *Anstalten*. These are really a kind of personal corporation. They can be capitalized at levels involving only a few thousand Swiss francs, the currency employed as legal tender by the principality. They are normally used as holding companies; that is, they are used to hold title to investments in other corporations (securities) or to bank deposits and the like. Normally, they are registered in the name of one of the lawyers or law firms in Liechtenstein (in either the capital, Vaduz, or Schaan). These lawyers are subject to a special code of secrecy that precludes them from revealing the identity of the true ownership behind these corporations. *Anstalten* are usually structured thus: bearer certificates of ownership are issued involving no registration whatsoever of beneficial ownership; the board of directors consists of one or two Liechtenstein lawyers; this board is given a power of attorney over the outstanding shares allowing them to make all decisions for the corporation. Usually there is also a side agreement with these lawyers precluding them from taking any steps without requesting specific permission from the beneficial owners.

It has been the practice for the *Anstalten* to enter agreements with the Liechtenstein authorities fixing the amount of tax to be paid in the future. Under such agreements it is possible that a corporation of this type will pay a maximum of 1,000 Swiss francs a year tax (less than $300), irrespective of its earnings and irrespective of its capitalization. There is a differentiation between the old type of *Anstalten*, usually those created before the mid-1960s, and the new ones. For the old ones, normally the fixed rate of taxation that has been agreed to by the state runs well into the 1980s and cannot be modified in the meantime. For the new *Anstalten* (those created after 1965), there is a possibility that a slight increase in the tax rate can be made in the mid-1970s. But any rate of corporate tax in Liechtenstein is, in even the worst case, infinitesimal compared to that in most other areas in the world.

Liechtenstein and its peculiar *Anstalten* have come under increasing criticism by tax authorities in a number of countries. It is claimed that such Liechtenstein corporations are used to hide the true ownership of funds running into billions of dollars, and evade the payment of any taxes whatsoever on the income accruing from such assets. The Swiss government is extremely careful in granting any privileges to *Anstalten* in Liechtenstein since it feels that many of its residents are using them as a cover. The United States has been trying to exert pressure on

Liechtenstein to lift its secrecy blanket regarding financial transactions. Thus far it has had no success whatever. However, as a consequence of this shadow hanging over Liechtenstein in recent years, it has lost some of its former popularity as a financial and tax haven.

Limit Orders. See Buy Orders and Sell Orders

Limit Up, Limit Down

Restrictions that commodity exchanges in the United States have put on the maximum upward or downward movement allowed in the price of a commodity during one daily trading session. The purpose of these controls is to prevent a total collapse of the market or, conversely, to preclude the price of any given commodity suddenly going out of sight upside. There is a selfish reason for the imposition of such limits up and limits down: they allow the brokers who handle commodity contracts to demand additional cash margins from those clients who find themselves on the wrong side of the market (see **Margin**). It's hard for new commodity investors to grasp the concept, for it's like saying General Motors will not be allowed to rise or fall more than three points in any one day. The reason it is so necessary in commodities is that these are virtually always bought on a big credit base. Hence limits are needed for the protection of both client and broker. The need for them serves to illustrate how risky the commodity market is: a day's movement can threaten to wipe out one's (margined) position.

Line and Bar Charts

Stock-market charts, drawn on either arithmetical paper or logarithmic paper, where the prices of the stock are posted to show the highest and lowest price of the day (or week, etc.) joined as a vertical line, and the closing price as a horizontal bar. These charts normally also show the volume of transactions at the bottom of the graph or chart. Principal alternative methods are charts that post only the closing price, and **point and figure charts** (see).

LINE AND BAR METHOD OF CHARTING

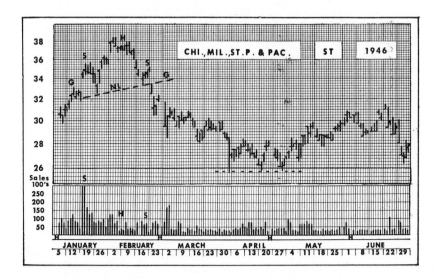

Liquidity, International

The amount of internationally acceptable funds in the world monetary system, in aggregate. Normally, international liquidity is the sum of gold, dollars, and, of late, SDRs (see **Special Drawing Rights**) available in aggregate as international reserves. In the 1960s, a major debate centered on the supposition that while world trade was expanding at a very rapid rate, international liquidity was lagging behind and, if not increased, would be insufficient for further growth. This led to the creation in 1968 of a new type of international liquidity, Special Drawing Rights, which were issued by the IMF as a paper substitute for gold. However, at the end of the 1960s the situation changed completely. As a result of the massive and continuing balance-of-payments deficits of the United States, the rest of the world was flooded with dollars, and there was an excess of international liquidity. It also triggered international inflation. This situation, it appears, will continue for a good number of years since there are no signs that the problems of the United States in regard to its balance of payments are being solved, and there is no plan underway for mopping up the excess liquidity in the form of excess dollars already existing in the world monetary system.

Liquidity, National

Term used to describe the monetary situation within a country as measured by its interest rates on deposits and loans. Liquidity is said to be bad if it is difficult to get a loan and the interest one is forced to pay on it is high. Liquidity is good (i.e., money is abundant in banks) if loans are easy and the rates low. Correspondingly, of course, as loan interest rises, so does deposit interest, and so people are encouraged to save, taking money out of circulation. Controlling how much money circulates and how freely it circulates is a favorite government activity, as a magic formula to solve any economic ill that happens to arise. (Also see **Liquidity, International** and **Liquidity, Personal or Corporate.**)

Liquidity, Personal or Corporate

The quality or state of possessing liquid assets that is, *cash* or assets that can be quickly converted into cash. (See also **Liquidity, International** and **Liquidity, National**.)

Loan, Term. See **Term Loan**

Lombard Credit and Lombard Rate

The term "Lombard credit" or "Lombard loan" is generally restricted to the continent of Europe. The word "Lombard" goes back to the Lombardy region of Italy, where this type of loan was first introduced by Italian bankers in the sixteenth century. Essentially a Lombard loan or advance is nothing more than an advance against the collateral of specific listed securities. The general practice is for banks to extend credit of up to 50 percent of the market value of such securities. The rate of interest charged on this type of loan, called the Lombard rate, tends to be fairly low since the collateral can be converted into cash on very short notice in the securities markets.

Long

An investor is "long" when he has *bought* stocks and holds them in the expectation that the price of such stocks or securities will go up. Another phrasing is to say "he is long the market" or "I am long GM"

(General Motors). The opposite is to "short," which refers to an advance-selling process, wherein you hope prices will fall. (See **Short Sale**.)

Luxembourg

A small principality bordered by France, Belgium, and West Germany; it is now a financial "island." Only in recent years has it become a relatively important financial center, chiefly because of special tax considerations allowed by Luxembourg to corporations, especially in regard to their issuance of securities. In most countries in Western Europe there are tax withholdings on dividends paid out by corporations, usually in the range of 25 to 30 percent, plus various types of taxes imposed at the time of issue of securities. In Luxembourg, *neither* type of tax is applied. During the past ten years it has become extremely common for multinational corporations to establish subsidiary companies in Luxembourg that are employed as a vehicle through which to issue Eurocurrency bonds and, especially, Eurodollar bonds and convertible debentures. Most recently, bonds denominated in Luxembourg francs have become popular. These bonds are completely free of any Luxembourg tax either on the capital at issue or on any dividends or capital distribution paid out later. A further advantage of Luxembourg is that it is extremely flexible in regard to allowing securities to be quoted on the National Luxembourg Exchange. This means that it is possible to get official listing and official market prices in Luxembourg for even relatively small companies and relatively small issues almost immediately after issue. Still another advantage of Luxembourg as a financial center has been the strength of its currency. Luxembourg issues its own franc but only for internal use. Where international transactions are concerned, the Luxembourg and Belgium francs are identical. In the currency readjustment in 1971 the Belgium-Luxembourg franc was revalued upward rather considerably and is regarded as one of the stronger currencies in Western Europe.

Another feature of the Luxembourg financial community is that it originates the issue of bonds denominated in so-called European units of account simultaneously in a *group* of the hard European currencies, such as the West German mark and the Swiss, Belgian, and French francs and so forth. The owner of such bonds has protection against widespread currency risk in that, under the rules governing European unit-of-account bonds, interest and capital repayment are made in the currency that is devalued least—the currency that has best retained its value over the length of the bond issue. It is probable that the use of the unit-of-account technique will greatly spread in coming years as more and more international financing, and especially long-term financing through the issue of securities, will be done in non-U.S. dollar terms.

About six major banks are domiciled in Luxembourg, all of which do the regular type of commercial banking business, such as accepting deposits and making loans to business and commerce, as well as investment banking and brokerage. They offer facilities to the international investor almost as complete as those offered by Swiss banks. Luxembourg bankers in general are fluently multilingual and are able to deal with customers in English, German or French. The secrecy laws of Luxembourg banks are not so tight as those in Switzerland but nevertheless offer an appreciable measure of confidentiality. Luxembourg also has allowed complete freedom of movement in the realm of currency exchange, which can be advantageous to international investors employing the facilities of banks in that principality. One of the disadvantages of Luxembourg as a center for the operations of a private international investor is the difficulties related to travel and communications. One must go there either by train from Brussels or by car or by a small propeller airplane operated by Lux Air. The Luxembourg government is trying to promote Luxembourg as one of the future financial centers in the European Economic Community and is attracting more and more international banks, especially those from the United States and West Germany. However, viewed realistically, it seems fated to remain a relatively small financial center, used more for the special tax advantages it offers than for any other purpose.

Macro Economics

This deals with national economic aggregates, such as gross national product and national income. (See also **Micro Economics**.)

Majority

One speaks of a majority in a corporation when more than 50 percent of the shares of that company are controlled by one person or group.

Unless there are very special circumstances, this person or group has essential control of the corporation.

Margin

A small, high-cost loan from your broker. When you buy stock on margin you cannot take possession of the certificates; they are technically your property but are held by the brokerage house when you buy the stock as security against your margin debt. The lure of margin is that you can buy more stock for the same money, and the prospect of owning more stock that is likely to go up is attractive. But there is also more stock to *lose* money on should it go down, and if the stock goes down, *fast,* the risk is acute that you will be sold out by the brokerage house and lose everything invested. Margin rights, which determine the amount of money you must put up and are expressed as a percentage of the credit you are allowed, have varied over the years. In 1929 they were about 10 percent which many people say is why 1929 was so sharp at the top: there were too many people being sold out by brokers when their stock dropped a mere few points, for they literally ran out of money. These days margin requirements in the United States range between 50 and 80 percent. It is against the law for a bank to lend you money to buy stock, which is why the broker can charge you a loan rate higher than the bank's and get away with it—he has almost a monopoly on that particular loan market. (See also **Margin Call**.)

Margin Call

Usually it is possible to buy a security or commodity on margin, i.e., by only a down payment of a certain percentage of the price of the security or commodity, with the broker advancing the remaining amount for the customer. If the market value of the security or commodity falls below the margin level, the bank or broker sends out a *margin call* to the client requesting that he replenish the difference between the purchase price and current market price. Failure to answer the margin call with fresh funds will cause the broker to "sell him out." If the broker can't reach his client and the price continues to fall, the broker will normally sell him out automatically unless there is a special relationship and a foreknowledge of the client's wishes in such an event.

Mark. See **Deutsche Mark**

Market if Touched (M.I.T.) Orders. See **Buy Orders and Sell Orders**

Market Orders. See **Buy Orders and Sell Orders**

Mental Stops. See **Buy Orders and Sell Orders**

Merchant Bank

In general, a term restricted to England. There, a merchant bank is defined as an institution that is normally occupied with underwriting securities for corporate clients, advising corporations on mergers and acquisitions, and participating in ownership of commercial enterprises. The famous merchant banks are Rothschild's, Hambro's, Montague's, and S. G. Warburg.

Micro Economics

This deals with the economics of a company or a market, and specifically with supply, demand, and price of single products.

Milliard. See **Billion**

Minerva

(Tax haven to be?) The world's newest country, built up from a coral reef in the South Pacific by a group of Americans, disenchanted with the ways of today's America. The group, under the inspiration of Michael Oliver, is seeking to found several new nations, wherever they can obtain land and sovereignty, to be based on the original U.S. Constitution, which they contend is no longer followed but has been gutted by Amendments and Supreme Court rulings. Minerva, as much as a place, is a symbol of new mini-nations to come that will operate under as pure a form of capitalism and laissez-faire as is possible, with hard, gold-backed money and virtually no government. There will be no president, no taxes, and strict control over immigration to keep out undesirables. Further information may be obtained from Mr. Oliver at P.O. Box 485, Reno, Nev. 89701.

Mines and Oils

A chart service on Canadian mining and oil companies. Published weekly by Frazer Research, 159 Bay Street, Toronto 1, Ontario. $55 per year.

Mining Journal

A unique publication, covering all South African gold mines and their shares, and providing in-depth coverage of these corporations' quarterly reports. It gives not only full statistics regarding the mining operations but also full financial coverage, including what is happening in regard to share prices and the like. The *Mining Journal* does not restrict itself to a simple recitation of facts and figures but ventures opinions regarding the suitability of mining shares for investment at any given time. Very high quality. Published monthly. Address *Mining Journal*, 15 Wilson Street, London E.C.2., England. Price $18.25 a year by air to the United States.

Minority

A shareholder or group of shareholders having less than 50 percent of the outstanding shares of the corporation. The share participation of a minority group is always of a noncontrolling nature.

Monaco

A small principality on the Mediterranean, with all its land frontiers joining France. Monaco consists of three towns: Monaco, La Condamine, and Monte Carlo (of casino fame). It is about two miles long and a half mile wide, and its government is a hereditary limited monarchy. Monaco is a tax haven. There is *no* personal income tax once you have established residency, provided you are not French. But individuals who are in business and who derive 25 percent of their gross income from outside Monaco are subject to profit tax on "net" of 35 to 40 percent.

Money Market

General term for a financial market in which currencies are loaned out or borrowed on a relatively short-term basis, and on an interbank or interinstitutional level. Normally the maturities of loans and borrowings in the money market are one year or less. This term is employed generally only in connection with transactions involving fairly substantial sums of money, for instance $100,000 and up. Negotiable certificates of deposit, acceptances, and commercial paper are the type of instruments commonly handled in the money market.

Monte Carlo. See Monaco

Month Orders. See Buy Orders and Sell Orders

Mortgage Bond

Bond guaranteed or backed through a mortgage on land or other real estate (houses, plants, etc.) In theory they are the safest bonds; for if the company goes broke, the bondholders can collectively claim against the property as collateral. In practice this often isn't so; for if a real estate company goes bust, the chances are that the properties it owns have dropped badly in value, making the bonds worth much less than when issued.

Moving Average

A method of ironing out the minor fluctuations in any stock-market indicator in order to produce a general trend. First one must decide what sort of trend one requires. If you are interested in trading on a short-term basis, such as weekly, then a *weekly* moving average of a stock price movement is relevant. You add up the daily prices in the past week, then divide by the number of days involved (usually five in this case). Each day thereafter you add the latest day and subtract the earliest one, and redivide the number to continue an average that moves along. This is in many ways a more sensitive way of plotting prices and statistics than merely taking, say, the weekend price and making a straight weekly chart. It has the advantage of smoothing out all except the unusually large (and therefore significant) daily fluctuations.

Mutual Fund

A financial institution that sells issues and certificates to the general public and invests the proceeds in an assortment of shares of public corporations. The term indicates the mutuality of ownership among a large group of private investors. The rationale of the mutual fund rests on the fact that it is practically impossible for the usual private investor by himself to achieve true diversification. It would be too difficult for him, and probably too expensive in terms of brokerage fees, to spread his investments over a large group of corporations. By pooling the funds of many small investors, mutual funds can achieve this objective of risk-spending. It is also possible for a mutual fund to gain the advice of expert investment advisers, people to whom the small private investor simply would not have access. The fees charged the purchaser of mutual-fund shares vary widely. A few years ago most mutual funds charged about 9 percent, and a few of them charged a "front-end loading fee," which meant most of one's initial payments went for commissions. Today fees are generally lower, and many "no-load" (no-fee) funds are flourishing. Performance varies widely, and funds that do well one year often slip the next. Some funds specialize in a single industry, but most are general. Collectively they are a major source of buying power in the market. They are equally a major potential source of selling power, for their holdings are large and they may either decide to sell or be forced to sell by investor redemption of their share certificates. In British usage mutual funds are called *unit trusts*.

For the investor with above average know-how, mutual funds are not considered an attractive investment, for the following reasons: 1) They are, after all, managed by men. Some perform better than the market and some perform worse; some perform better than the market one year and a lot worse the next. You cannot be sure you are buying the right fund at the right time. 2) Buying a fund lulls you into a sense of complacency that you have made your investment and you can forget it. This could prove a disaster at turning points in the market, for these funds represent large bodies of money and therefore are much less maneuverable than the individual investor. They cannot move into or out of stocks as quickly as you can privately. 3) They are usually not tailored to your individual needs as an investor. Their stock selection is the same for widows and orphans as they are for up-and-coming executives, even though the needs of these two groups are different. 4) They have to be *more* right than you would be, doing it alone, since for their services they take a percentage, which means that in order to just break even for you, they have to win back that percentage first. To summarize: to buy a mutual fund is like buying a stock at a premium. You must first make up for the premium, and with those built-in odds against you the funds should be a lot more right than their records generally show. Also, in times of severe crisis you may even have trouble turning your fund shares into cash (witness I.O.S. and GRAMCO), whereas you can always sell your own individual stock at some sort of price.

Even so, the funds have their proper place in the investment spectrum, for they provide a method of diversified and supervised investing for those unable or unwilling to make their own decisions. Funds tend to be used by very small investors, those who do not participate in the stock market in any other way. (See also **Offshore Funds; Performance Funds**.)

Nationalization

The taking over of ownership of a company or an industry by the state. Under Communism all enterprise belongs to the government. In the West, nationalization in most countries occurs infrequently and often on a limited scale. Sometimes a government takes over an industry when the owners cannot make it pay (e.g., transportation), whereupon the government pours money into it to keep the laws of supply and demand from running their course and causing the industry to close and throw numbers of people out of work. The problem with such moves is that almost invariably the industry does worse under government control than it did under private enterprise; therefore, instead of helping, the take-over makes the situation worse. More and more money has to be pumped into the industry, which indirectly thus raises the tax bill of the country. The employees of the industry are living off the state as surely as if they were on social security. The first thing many of the newly independent countries in Africa did was to nationalize all or some major industries, which in effect was direct seizure of businesses that were owned and prospering under white ex-imperial nations, and then to inject home rule into the management, invariably with disastrous results. Nationalization changes all employees of a company or industry into "civil servants." If governments had been as all-pervasive in the early 1900s as they are today, perhaps they would have taken over the failing manufacture of buggy whips and still be making them today.

Socialist-leaning people tend to feel that it is somehow more "fair" for government to own things like utilities, airlines, and big industry, so that the benefits are spread over the population more evenly. But there is scant evidence to indicate that government-run businesses can make as much profit as those run by private citizens, and in fact they more often run at losses. The people at large lose in several ways, mainly through the loss of the taxes formerly paid by those industries to government. They also end up having to subsidize losses and, worst of all, often get a lower quality of service since the attitude of civil servants throughout the world is less oriented toward helping the customer than is that of the workers in private enterprise. Privately owned telephone companies, for example, in general provide better, more pleasant service and net the government more money in taxes than government telephone systems. The case for nationalization is a poor one, yet there seem few publicists able and willing to articulate the case for private enterprise.

Netherlands

One of the major European financial centers for centuries. The city of **Amsterdam** (see) is generally recognized as its financial capital. Dutch banks, like their counterparts in Switzerland and Germany, are universal banks. That is, they not only accept deposits and make loans to business and industry as commercial banks but are also very active in the field of securities, acting as brokers for clients or as underwriters for corporations. The Amsterdam Stock Exchange, one of the oldest in the world, is the center of trading for a number of very important international stocks such as Royal Dutch and Philips. The Dutch guilder has emerged as one of Europe's hard currencies; during the worldwide currency readjustment of 1971 it was revalued upward relative to the American dollar by more than 10 percent. The Netherlands banking system especially offers very convenient facilities for the average international investor, particularly to those from Anglo-Saxon countries, for people in the Dutch banking system or in the financial community in general seem as much at home in the English language as they are in their own. The facilities offered by Dutch banks compare quite favorably to those offered by banks in Switzerland. To be sure, the Dutch banking system does not have a system of secrecy laws such as those existing in Switzerland. Nevertheless it is generally recognized that for efficiency the Dutch banks rank as high as any in the world.

Netherlands Antilles

A relative newcomer to the tax-haven business, and one that is keenly interested in attracting new customers. Formerly a Caribbean Dutch colony, it is now a coequal part of the Kingdom of the Netherlands, with a popularly elected legislature. It offers the standard tax-haven type of company for holding other companies, patents, copyrights, etc., outside the islands. A holding company is taxed at 2.4 percent on net profits not exceeding $50,000 and 3 percent on profits over that. There is no surtax or capital-gains tax. Each corporation can be guaranteed these rights for ten years. There are no withholding taxes or estate duty. Used by multinational companies and private citizens alike.

Neue Zürcher Zeitung

Leading daily newspaper of Switzerland. Its language is German, and it comes out in three separate daily editions from its headquarters in Zurich. It is a conservative newspaper generally staunchly opposed to Communism and the policies of Communist countries and also generally friendly toward the United States. Its business and economics section is regarded as a must by financial people in Central Europe in order to keep up with developments not only in Switzerland but throughout the continent. *Neue Zürcher Zeitung's* coverage of financial events in Germany, France, Italy, Benelux, the United Kingdom, and the United States is probably unparalleled in any other newspaper in depth and scope. *Neue Zürcher Zeitung* publishes a biweekly summary in English of what its editorial staff considers to be the most important articles of the prior two weeks. However in most cases such articles deal with political rather than financial or economic events.

New Deal

Phrase coined by President Franklin D. Roosevelt for his economic programs introduced in the 1930s. The most important features of the New Deal were programs designed to combat unemployment in the United States and to regenerate growth at the time of the Great Depression. The New Deal had many social (some people would term them socialistic) aspects since it was under the New Deal that social security, taxation systems penalizing the well-to-do, and many bodies designed to control and police corporate activity were introduced. The New Deal has in many respects been identified with the economic concepts of John Maynard Keynes. Part and parcel of the New Deal was pump priming, or deficit spending, by the United States government as a means to step up demand and thus create a general upward economic spiral. The inauguration of the New Deal signaled the separation of the United States fiscal and monetary policy from the conservatism of prior years. For instance, Roosevelt abandoned the concept of linking money in circulation to gold. He abandoned the concept of having balanced budgets. He created a general framework that has since led to a stupendous growth in the national debt of the United States. Many observers feel that the New Deal established the basis for inevitable high rates of inflation in the United States through the readiness of the federal government to create more and more money involving more and more deficits leading to ever higher rates of price increases. In retrospect some feel that perhaps some kind of New Deal was inevitable in the 1930s in order to check the development of possible serious revolutionary unrest at that time, but others think it was the wrong medicine. In any case, its adoption marked a new phase in the economic development of the United States.

It is important today for international private investors to recognize a new trend similar to that back in the 1930s. Today, high rates of inflation produced by federal spending programs and general fiscal irresponsibility, it becomes more and more difficult for people who save their money to protect its purchasing power. One of the investor's *prime* objectives today must be to find ways of conserving his capital against the erosion of inflation. Many have thought that they could do this in the stock market; but as history (especially in the 1960s) proved, these hopes were illusory. More and more people have turned to investments in such things as real estate, gold, shares in gold mines, investment situations in countries with relatively low rates of inflation, and investments in the countries with the highest growth rates (e.g., Japan). In the late 1960s and early 1970s it became clear to investors that high rates of inflation produced by government spending programs must also lead to international deterioration in the value of the dollar and to dollar devaluations. The prudent investor in the United States today more and more seeks international diversification of his assets as a hedge against the effects of government economic policy, dating back to the New Deal, upon his money and savings.

New York Stock Exchange (NYSE)

The biggest-volume stock exchange in the world. The shares of most of the major corporations in the United States are traded here. The beginnings of the New York Stock Exchange go back to the year 1792, when twenty-four brokers gathered under a tree in Wall Street to trade the first "public stocks." In 1817 they put together a set of rules and adopted New York Stock Exchange. Only three times in the history of the NYSE has it had to be closed: in 1873 during a financial crisis, in 1914 with the outbreak of the First World War, and in 1933 as a result of the general bank moratorium declared by the federal government for the entire country. It has been located since 1922 at 11 Wall Street, a location which has made that street synonymous with investment and high finance in all languages of the world. The NYSE has approximately 1,400 members, of whom about a quarter are called *specialists*. These are the men on the floor of the exchange who restrict themselves to trading one or a very small number of stocks. They serve as the center for trading in the stocks in which they specialize; they also act as price moderators in that they *always* stand prepared to make a deal in the securities in which they are specialists. A seat on the N.Y. Stock Exchange can be bought in the free market. The price of these seats has been subject to substantial fluctuation. In 1929, as much as $625,000 was paid for a seat. In 1942, the price had sunk to $17,000. At present seats are selling in the range of $250,000 to $300,000.

The exchange is governed by a board of directors, which elects a chairman. There are thirty-three board members, including the president, who is hired by the exchange as its chief executive officer. The exchange is open Monday through Friday between 10 A.M. and 3:30 P.M. The trading floor is organized around nineteen separate so-called trading posts, at which the specialists (for groups of stocks) are centered. A specialist "makes a market" that is always available for buying or selling the shares in which he specializes, to the brokers who gather on the floor of the exchange to execute buy and sell orders for their clients. The NYSE provides more data about trading than any other stock exchange by far. Simple things like daily volume in each stock are unobtainable in most countries. Accurate data on the daily high and low prices of each stock are also not available to investors outside the New York market. The London Stock Exchange is larger in the *number* of shares listed and in the broad spectrum of countries covered, but information about price and volume is virtually a secret, seemingly to be kept from the customers. This is probably because technical analysis is not widely popular outside the United States, though it is gaining ground. The NYSE is virtually a symbol of the United States, and/or of the dollar, and/or capitalism at (perhaps) its best.

Objets d'Art

Pronounced "obe-jay dar." A French term meaning art objects, including everything from paintings to statues, from antiques to rare plates, from delicate vases to old glassware. Are they a good investment? Views differ, mainly because few collectors are also economists. Probably the answer is that it depends on what kind of business climate prevails. Let's take three different climates: 1) The normal boom and recession cycle. Here prices of art rise with the boom and fall with the recession. One profits if buying early and selling before prices peak. One can easily lose if buying a bit late and finding after a peak that there are no buyers in a shrinking market. 2) The inflation syndrome. Here prices in general just go on rising; and as long as they do, art objects get more valuable. If a money squeeze occurs during inflation, there may be few buyers for art, which would make art nonliquid. But overall, art is safe to hold as long as no end is seen to the inflation trend. In climate No. 1 we presume no notable inflation. In climate No. 2 we presume nothing about business, which could vary considerably.

For climate No. 3 we'll assume a combination of No. 1 and No. 2— a boom-recession cycle laced with inflation. This comes closest to the conditions of recent times. When a general boom was on, art objects rose so spectacularly for reasons of boom and inflation that, as a type of investment, they had been called *the biggest gainers on earth*. Old-master prints rose by severalfold *per year* in some years. But then the business boom peaked and art slipped a bit. Classically, inflation will prevent their prices from falling too much (for at such times people cling to "stores of values"), while a down business cycle can keep them from rising, or from rising very much. Art holders must decide in the latter half of this third climate whether inflation is accelerating or declining, while business is stagnating or being indecisive. *While inflation increases, art can be held. When it starts to flag, art must be quickly sold. Waiting for peak prices is fatal* because a money squeeze can develop *before* inflation ends, and buyers will be unavailable regardless of "values." The worst of all situations for art is when inflation turns to deflation at the same time a business recession takes hold. Then prices fall for two valid reasons, and they fall very fast. It is especially so because art is a luxury, not a necessity. Thus art collections must always sell "too soon" in order to sell *at all*. But while inflation rages unchecked, they can hang on blissfully. A bonus with art is that one can enjoy looking at it, irrespective of value. There's no such joy from bonds.

Odd-Lot Index

Index of the activity of so called odd-lotters, that is the purchases and sales of lots of stock smaller than the standard hundred-share lot and hence usually the activity of the small or very small investor. In odd-lot theory it is maintained that the odd-lotter can be right in mid-trend but is wrong at turning points. Therefore if the odd-lotter suddenly becomes a heavy net purchaser, this is interpreted as a sign that a bull trend is peaking out. If, on the other hand, in the process of a bear trend the odd-lotters finally become heavy net sellers and also sell short abnormally, this would generally be interpreted as a sign that a turn-around in general market conditions could be expected. The premise for this interpretation of the behavior of small investors is an assumption that has been generally accepted and was for some time at least probably true: that the small investor is particularly apt to get caught up in the final emotional stages of bull- or bear-market psychology, while the professional trader, armed with much more experience and equipped with better information and advice, is able to maintain his objectivity.

In recent years the behavior of the odd-lotters seems to have taken on a bearish bias, and a number of stock-market observers no longer feel that the historical interpretation of their behavior is valid. However, despite their bias of selling on balance, the odd-lot figures can probably still be interpreted on a *relative* basis with some validity. It is important to remember that the common concept that the odd-lotters are always wrong is incorrect. Rather it is when they act differently from their own norm, when they gang up at the exits or entrances to the stock market, that they are wrong, because no market of any kind can accommodate onesidedness without producing a reversal.

Offshore Funds

For Americans, a term for mutual funds headquartered outside the United States or off its shores. They became especially important in the mid-1960s. The objective of offshore funds was to provide a vehicle for investment in growth situations through the acquisition of securities, usually stocks of non-American corporations. In general, the certificates of offshore funds are not legally available to citizens of the United States but are sold to investors in Western Europe and Latin America. The peculiarity of offshore funds is that, although they depend upon non-American investment situations, for the most part the fund managers have been American, who have attempted to bring the philosophy and expertise of the immense American mutual-fund industry to other countries. Offshore funds managed by American groups have had a very spotty record at best. Quite often they invested in situations of which they had insufficient knowledge. They often overinvested in particular countries or in particular high-risk sectors of industry and commerce.

Their performance was generally so poor that most of them have either been closed down or are now operating at a very low level. In general the international investing public became quite disillusioned with this type of financial vehicle. Today Europeans have for the most part turned to mutual funds managed by nationals of their own country and operated according to European standards.

Open-Market Operations

Acts of intervention by the central bank of a country in that country's capital market, specifically the bond market. Open-market operations are essentially employed to control the supply of funds in the capital market and thus to control interest rates. In its simplest form it works like this: if a central bank such as the Federal Reserve System in the United States desires to inject money into the system it will appear as a *purchaser* of government bonds in the market, buying these bonds from the country's commercial banks. What this does in effect is to give such banks increased liquidity, which allows them to be more liberal in making loans. If the policy is pushed far enough, the liquidity of the commercial banking system will become so great that competition between the banks will result in a general lowering of interest rates on a nationwide scale. Conversely, when the central bank desires to reduce liquidity, it will appear as a *seller* of government bonds, thus sopping up the excess liquidity (i.e., cash) in the banking system, replacing cash with interest-bearing government bonds. It is generally recognized that open-market operations are a quite effective short-term means for the United States government to influence the interest rates and general credit situation within the country.

It is of great importance for the private investor to follow the open-market operations of his government or of the central bank of his country. If it becomes apparent that the government is working toward a general lowering of interest rates through open-market operations, obviously bonds, both government and industrial, will become increasingly attractive, since the price of bonds goes in an inverse direction to the movement of interest rates. Liberalization of liquidity in the commercial banking system is normally also bullish for industry, since it will allow businessmen to borrow money and expand their operations at better terms than earlier. This in the longer term can be a bullish factor for stock markets. Conversely, when the central bank is sopping up liquidity through open-market operations, this indicates that the government is aiming for a general tightening up of credit conditions and perhaps for a slowdown in the overall economic growth of the country in the immediate future. This would in general make bonds unattractive, as interest rates are going to rise; and it would likewise, with a time lag, mean that the growth potential for corporations and their stocks would be limited until these brakes were once again removed.

Orders to Brokers. See **Buy Orders and Sell Orders**

Ordinary Share

British term for what in the United States is called a *common share* or *common stock*.

Overbought-Oversold Index

The form of this index most commonly used is a ten-day moving average of the difference between advances and declines. When a market moves down too fast, some people sell not for valid reasons but from fright. Thus declines pile up and an oversold condition results; that is, panic selling has caused the market to move down further than valid fundamental market conditions justify, and so a correction is to be expected. The same happens on the advance when euphoria gets the better of the investing public, and stocks sell for much higher prices than they are worth. In actual figures, about plus 1,200 is considered overbought territory and minus 1,600 is considered oversold. But remember this index, like all market indexes, is merely a guide to market behavior; none of them are magic tools to win the speculation war. The drawback to any kind of overbought or oversold index is that there is nothing to prevent a market from getting *more* oversold after it is already in oversold territory (or more overbought). The best use of the index is merely to let you know when a reversal is due in a broad sense. No specific timing day can be determined from this index. It is also of more use during undramatic market conditions. When a market crashes, the index is useless because it is oversold almost from the start and just stays that way, day after day, as the market plummets. To buy stocks because this index says the market is oversold during a severe downturn could be folly.

OVERBOUGHT-OVERSOLD INDEX

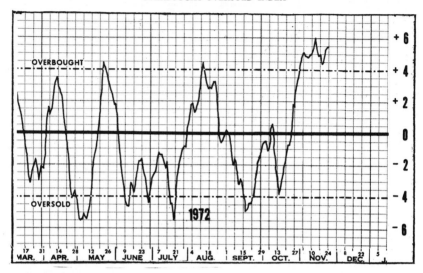

Overdraft

Borrowings by a bank's private client by his overdrawing his account. The overdraft system is especially common in England. Generally it works this way: the bank manager, after scrutinizing the personal assets of a client, will establish an overdraft limit. At any time it will be the privilege of the client to overdraw his account up to that limit, and he will normally pay a rate of interest on this overdraft at two or three percentage points above the bank rate or discount rate. It is also normal that on a regular basis the client should reduce the loan he got by his overdraft to zero and build up a positive balance in his account. The advantage of the overdraft system is that it allows people to borrow money easily and readily on a short-term basis, without having to resort to complicated loan agreements and the like.

Overnight Money. See Call Money

131

OVER-THE-COUNTER MARKET

Over-the-Counter Market (OTC)

In the United States, the noninstitutionalized market for securities, that is, the trading of securities outside the framework of the New York Stock Exchange, the American Stock Exchange, or any other U.S. exchange. The over-the-counter market in the United States embraces tens of thousands of stocks of small, even very small companies, often of only regional importance. Because of the noninstitutionalized trading, most OTC stocks are highly volatile. Often only a very limited number of shares change hands in one day or even one week. Thus if a buyer comes in for the purpose of acquiring a block, he may find it extremely difficult and have to contact many different brokerage companies throughout the country in order to find a willing seller or sellers. Also, as a result of his activity the price of the stock may go up appreciably. Still, the over-the-counter market, despite its volatility and despite the fact it is not policed in the same manner as the NYSE or the ASE, should be constantly under surveillance by private investors. Quite often the superstars of tomorrow have their beginnings in the OTC market of today. That was the case for many companies in the electronics or computer field that are now among the most highly graded stocks on the New York Stock Exchange—they could have been bought many years ago as insignificant companies in the OTC market. Some brokerage houses specialize in certain OTC stocks. These are often the houses which initially sponsored the underwriting of these stocks, first bringing the shares of these corporations into the hands of the public. If one desires to engage in the trading of a specific OTC stock, it is recommended that a relationship be established with the brokerage house that specializes in it, since there and often only there can one get the necessary information both on the company and on the market for its stock, enabling an investor to make sound investment decisions. This may also be the best place to sell it.

One should not make the mistake of regarding the OTC market as containing *only* small companies. Some firms prefer to be OTC. The insurance companies, for example, are almost all OTC, and they are among the biggest corporations in the land. Prices for OTC stocks are found on "pink sheets" in brokerage offices, and selected lists of OTC stocks appear in various newspapers, including the *Wall Street Journal,* and in *Barron's* magazine. There are more stocks in the OTC market than in all the stock exchanges of the United States combined.

Panama

Latin-American tax haven, as half the shipping lines of the world will tell you. Ships and shipping lines register in Panama because of its favorable shipping regulations on import and export. There is no income tax or corporation tax on income derived outside Panama. There is no tax on bank interest. Taxes on nonresident companies are, as in most tax havens, virtually nonexistent. Added to this, Panama has banking secrecy and will offer you a numbered account in any popular currency.

Paris Bourse

National stock exchange of France. It was founded on September 24, 1724, on the basis of a decree of the government. In 1807, the Code du Commerce created the basis for the legal status of brokers (called *Agents de Change*) who were given the exclusive right to trade in securities and to establish the price of securities. The number of Agents de Change is today fixed at 85. They have a double status: they are both officials of the government (in French, *officiers ministériels*) and private traders. They are appointed by the Minister of Finance and are subject to stringent examinations and regulations. A new Agent de Change can be nominated only by his predecessor or, in the case of a death of an Agent de Change, by his heirs. In addition to being nominated it is necessary that the candidate have the backing of the Chambre Syndicale. If he secures this, the seat on the Bourse is transferred to him at a price fixed by the Chambre Syndicale. He must deposit a guarantee for fulfillment of his obligations under the rules of the exchange.

The Agent de Change is not only responsible in regard to trading proper but also is obliged to carry through all the financial transactions related to the transfer of shares from the seller to the buyer. This requires a good amount of working capital. It is usual for most brokerage firms in Paris to be organized as a kind of partnership, with silent partners contributing a good part of the necessary working capital. The Agents de Change are a very close-knit group of officials. Past practice indicates that if a broker finds himself in financial difficulties the Chambre

Syndicale will provide the necessary financial cover. The Chambre Syndicale uses for this purpose a so-called *"Fonds Commun,"* which is financed on a regular basis by deductions out of their brokerage fees and their annual profits.

The determination of prices on the Bourse in Paris is not exactly simple. Three different methods are employed: *criée, par opposition,* and *par casiers.* The method usually employed is the *criée,* in which the brokers gather around a ring and cry their bid and ask prices to each other across it. The problem with this type of trading is that it works very slowly; only about thirty different securities can be handled in the two hours provided each day for this type of trading. The brokers go down the list alphabetically, security by security, and trading continues in each share until all interests have been satisfied; then they move on to the second on the list and so forth. The second method of trading, *par opposition,* is done in the following manner: The bid and ask prices are established and published before the opening of the exchange by the Chambre Syndicale. These prices are to the so-called *côteurs.* During the trading hours of the exchange, specialists in different types of securities sit down with their colleagues and put together the various buy and sell orders they have. Somewhat as in a fixing process (see **Gold Fixing**), a fair price is arrived at and all transactions in a given security are then made at this price. The third method, *par casiers,* involves the establishment of the price through an Agent de Change. Each Agent de Change specializes in certain securities. He takes the buy and sell orders of his colleagues for a given stock, compares them with each other, and then sets a price, which is posted; all transactions in the stock that day are made *at this price.*

Most international observers consider the organization of the Paris exchange to be archaic; and it is not unlikely that a more viable system of trading will be developed in the future, in the pool of European economic integration, along the lines of those existing in New York or London. The Paris Bourse, although a very large number of shares are listed on it, has essentially never played a role as important in its country's economy as has the New York, London, Frankfurt, or Zurich exchange. It is a very thin market, where the buying or selling of any major block of shares can result in substantial price fluctuations. The underlying cause for the limitations of the Bourse as a financial factor in France is that share ownership has never developed a very broad base among the French people, a fact that makes it difficult for corporations to raise funds in the French equity market. Thus for French corporate finance, bonds and bank loans still remain the primary sources. It is probable that an increasing number of French corporations will bypass the Paris Bourse and seek to establish an active market for their shares in other financial centers, especially London, where a large investing public exists and where a corporation can raise substantial funds through new issues.

The private international investor has not been active in the past on the Paris Bourse. The reasons go back to the fact that, in general, financial information on French companies has been very sketchy and therefore it has been most difficult for a private investor, especially an international investor who lives outside France, to make a proper assessment of what he is buying. Another reason is that the market on the Paris Bourse in most shares is so thin that there is little scope for block buying and selling. The situation may gradually improve in the years ahead if the Paris Bourse is reorganized and especially if the ownership base in France proper is increased through the expansion of mutual funds. French mutual funds were introduced to the public in the 1960s and have been enjoying modest though growing popularity. Should their growth continue, it could mean a revival in the status and attractiveness of the Paris Bourse. International private investors who desire to explore the potential of French stocks are probably best advised first to contact their local home bank and be given advice on what bank in Paris can best look after their investment interest in France. Banks in France, especially the *banques d'affaires* (similar to British merchant banks), are heavily engaged in securities and security-portfolio management. Banks that specialize in securities are probably in the best position to provide an international investor with the type of company information he will require in order to develop a prudent investment program in that country.

Parity

The central exchange value of a currency. For example, the parity of a Swiss franc in September 1973 was 3.02 SwFr = $1.00. The actual exchange rate can fluctuate by 2.25 percent above or below this parity or central exchange value. (See **International Monetary Fund.**)

Participation Bonds

Also known as *Funding bonds*. The holders receive, in addition to the normal fixed interest on such bonds, a participation in the net profits of the issuing corporation.

Performance Funds

Mutual funds, especially in the 1960s, that sought to achieve *maximum capital growth* with the funds entrusted to them by many small private investors. Performance funds generally took much greater risks than other types of mutual funds, concentrating on so-called hot new issues and often on the shares of small unknown corporations in their attempt to achieve an outstanding "performance." The results of this type of investment proved disastrous in many instances, and in 1969 the fad faded.

Point and Figure Charts

A method of charting stock prices that differs from **line and bar charts** (see) because it takes no account of time or volume. Point and figure charts are plotted on equal-size-squared paper (arithmetical graph paper), and an "X" is posted to the chart each time the stock moves a full point up and an "O" for a down move of one full point. Some point and figure chartists use a five point move, and there are other variations too. Point and figure (P and F) charting is faster than line and bar, especially since on some days there will be nothing to post. P and F charting also saves space, for often several years of action can be shown on a sheet that would take several sheets for line and bar charting. Posting time per chart is also less, since it's much quicker to write an "X" or an "O" than to draw a high, a low, join them, and put in a crossbar, plus volume; the time factor is 500 percent more for line and bar charting. P and F is very good for determining price objectives in shares. It is also easier to see support and resistance levels. Its drawback probably lies in its insensitivity to short-term moves. Also, many feel the absence of volume to be an unfortunate limitation. However, P and F's proponents claim that volume is "built into" their plottings.

POINT AND FIGURE CHART

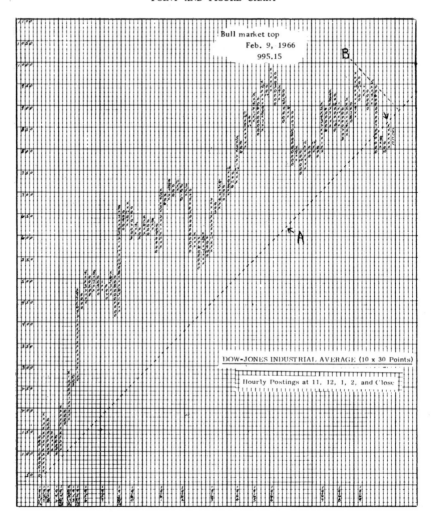

Chart courtesy Richard Russell, San Diego, Calif.

Pool

In stock-market circles, a group of speculators created for the purchase or sale of securities on the stock exchange, with the objective of manipulating the market price. The term is also used when a group of shareholders in a corporation enters into agreements under which they mutually agree to put their shares into a pool, usually under the condition that no single shareholder will sell his shares unless the entire grouping or pool make a block deal for their collective holdings in the company. This pool method is often employed to allow the founder of a corporation essentially to retain control over it; or (repeatedly in Europe) it may be used to protect the identity or nationality of someone who has control over a corporation. The word "pool" has also been used in regard to the gold bullion business. For example, prior to 1968 the major trading nations of the world formed a gold pool in London under which they pooled their resources, in the form of gold bullion. Out of this pool gold was then bought or sold on behalf of all the members of the pool on a pro rata basis, with the objective of stabilizing the gold price at $35 an ounce. When, as a result of speculative demand from the private sector, billions in gold bullion flowed out from these central banks' holdings to private investors, the London gold pool was disbanded.

Position

In banking circles, the standing of a bank customer in terms of total money value. For example, the elements of a customer's position may be assets such as shares, bonds, and real property, and liabilities such as a property mortgage and also perhaps an overdraft debt. Counted together, the pluses and minuses give the net *position* of that individual. In stock-market circles, to have a position in a stock means to own some of it. For example, if a person owns 100,000 shares of IBM, one can refer to this stock holding as his *position* in IBM. The same applies in foreign-exchange dealings. If a speculator has sold one million dollars against Swiss francs for three months forward delivery, one speaks of his having a short *position* in dollars and a long *position* in Swiss francs.

Postal Checking Systems

In continental Western Europe (in contrast to American and British practice), most settlements of debts between individuals or stores or even banks are not effected by means of personal checks but are made through the postal checking system. This is the prevailing way of making payments in such countries as West Germany, the Netherlands, Switzerland,

and France. In its simplest form it works in this way: assume that the lady of the house bought a dress from a shop and asked that the bill be sent. With its bill the shop would enclose a preprinted check indicating the amount owed and the number of their account in the postal checking service. Our lady goes to the post office at the end of the month and pays cash to be credited to that account. The post office gives her a receipt for this payment by tearing off a coupon from the check form and stamping it. It is also possible that if the household has a large number of such transactions, it will have a postal checking account. In that case, instead of paying cash over the counter the housewife will merely make a transfer from this P.O. checking account to the shop's checking account. The procedure is practically the same everywhere.

There is no charge to anyone for the processing of these payments through the postal checking system. However, no interest is paid on the balances in the accounts at the post office. This means, of course, that the post office system has a large amount of interest-free money or float, which it can apply to the money market. Thus for the most part the postal checking systems throughout Europe operate at a profit and still are able to provide a cost-free money-clearing service to the entire population. It usually goes under the name of Giro. It is being tried in England, with results as yet unavailable.

Postal Savings Service

Post offices or postal services in almost every country in Western Europe also offer savings plans. These are not to be confused with the postal checking systems, which are merely used to clear payments within the community. Postal savings services were established, mainly in the nineteenth century, to promote saving, especially saving with the security of the state behind one's deposits. Today in many countries this type of savings continues to provide major competition to other types of savings programs offered by the privately owned banking system, their interest rates comparing very favorably with that offered by private banking institutions.

Pound

The terms "pound" and "pound sterling" are employed to denote the currency of the United Kingdom. But "pound" is also employed to denote the currencies of other countries, including Ireland, Israel, Turkey, Egypt, Syria, Ghana, the Sudan, Libya, Lebanon, and New Zealand. The pound sterling is both the *major* currency with this name and the "mother" of the others. During the entire nineteenth century the pound sterling was far and away the most important currency in the world. The vast majority of foreign trade was conducted in terms of the pound, and the City of London was the financial capital of the world. As a result of the deterioration of the economic position of the United Kingdom following World War I and especially World War II, the pound decreased rapidly in importance. Today "only" 45 percent of world trade is settled in pound sterling, which has been displaced as No. 1 by the United States dollar in the post-World War II era. The pound sterling continues to serve as a reserve currency for many countries of the world, in particular some of those which are associated as Commonwealth members. In addition to holding gold, these countries employ sterling as a second international reserve, normally holding these reserves in London and receiving interest on them. The pound sterling has greatly decreased in international value during the past few decades. Once it cost $5 to acquire one pound. Today the rate is about half that figure. Many feel, however, that during the 1970s the series of sterling crises may ease and that finally the pound will be stabilized near its current international level. The pound (i.e., investment in the pound) offers some of the best yields on the international scene. For instance, on government securities denominated in pounds it is not unusual to get net yields of 8.5 to 9 percent per annum. Also, the London stock market, whose securities are of course denominated in pounds, is the world's second biggest in volume and is the largest in number of listed shares and countries represented. The turnover (volume) of the London Stock Exchange (securities denominated in pounds) is six times that of the turnover of all the German stock exchanges (securities denominated in German marks) on an annual basis. In the process of European economic integration, the pound sterling is being joined with the currencies of the original six members of the Common Market as one of the currencies in Europe used for intra-European settlement purposes. Many observers expect that, because of the preeminence of the London financial community and banking system, the pound sterling will end up with the leading role in future European monetary matters. Although this will not restore to the pound sterling the worldwide dominance it had in the nineteenth century, it would mean that its use as an international currency will no longer decline but will probably revive to a substantial degree (the origin of the word "pound" is the Latin "*pondus,*" meaning "weight"). "Sterling" of course springs from sterling silver. In the Carlovingian period, the Roman pound (twelve ounces) of pure silver was coined into 240 silver pennies. Hence the way the pound sterling was divided. The pound symbol (£) and the abbreviation "lb." are for *libra,* the Latin word for "pound."

Power of Attorney

Document assigning powers from one individual to another, enabling one to act on behalf of the other. Powers of attorney are often used in financial affairs. For instance, individuals who are not able to devote themselves to the day-to-day management of certain aspects of their financial affairs often give a power of attorney to their lawyer, enabling him to make decisions or take certain actions in specified areas on their behalf and to implement these decisions over his signature under the terms of the power of attorney granted to him. It's also not unusual, especially in Europe, for clients of a bank to grant power of attorney to their (bank) account executive. This enables the banking executive to trade securities for the client without the necessity of consulting him in regard to the buy and sell decisions. This method is quite often employed by international investors who live far from their bank and feel it prudent to give a power of attorney to their bankers in order to allow them to take quick on-the-spot actions should the situation require it.

Although there are many advantages to granting powers of attorney in the investment field, there are likewise a number of disadvantages that should be noted by investors. For example, unless very strict and specific guidelines are made part and parcel of the power of attorney, it can turn out that the individual who is allowed to manage the investments will operate according to objectives and risk concepts quite different from those of the owner of the funds. Therefore, in setting up powers of attorney, it is to be highly recommended that one give quite precise guidelines as to the areas of investment desired, the "mix" of the portfolio desired (for instance) as among interest-bearing bonds, capital notes, low-risk stocks, high-risk stocks, and the like, use of margin, etc. It is important that, should a power of attorney be granted to an investment adviser or banker, he be required to report regularly and completely on his activities to the owner of the funds. Generally this should be done at least each quarter.

The worst aspect of giving a power of attorney, especially in investments, is psychological. There is a subconscious tendency to assume that, when you give a power of attorney to someone this relieves you of all responsibility for your own assets. Somehow, too, the action may seem (in your mind) to endow the recipient of the POA with such great wisdom that whatever he does will surely enrich you. No one would ever say this aloud, but it does tend to take place in one's thinking. Since the premise is dangerous, one should never relax after granting a POA but should both monitor the situation and try to help the POA recipient. Nor is the latter ethically responsible for every subsequent event. He cannot know your situation as well as you, so he is more liable to make errors of judgment than you in certain areas at certain times. When arguments arise from unpleasant consequences of a POA, it is frequently because the person who gave it mistakenly assumed that his agent know what he wanted, what he would do in the same situation, what he could live with, what his reserve position was, and so on. Some feel it is debatable whether the risk of misunderstanding and wrong assumptions is worth taking. In any case, it's a matter for considerable thought before acting. A POA is like a wedding license; neither is a guarantee of happiness.

Precious Metals

A select group of metals such as gold, silver, platinum, and palladium. They are known as precious metals because they have been regarded as being of unusual value down through the ages.

Preference Shares (Preferred Stock)

Shares on which a dividend is paid out at a fixed rate before any dividend can be paid on the corporation's common shares. One must be careful not to equate preference or preferred shares with bonds. Bonds are instruments of debt under which the issuer is bound to pay the preagreed interest as long as it does not go into bankruptcy or make a special settlement with its debtors, whereas the payment of a dividend on preference shares is at the *option* of the corporation and depends generally on the annual profitability of the company. Quite often preferred shares are issued in so-called "cumulative form." This means that if, during a bad year (or a number of years), the dividend is not paid on the preferred shares at the prearranged rate, before any dividends are paid on the common shares the *cumulative* total of dividends not paid in the prior years must be paid first before the dividend can be paid on the common shares. Preferred shares are "redeemable" or "callable" when the corporation has the right to call them in, i.e., to take back the shares and pay back the subscription price and thus erase the obligation they embody from the company's books. One speaks of a "convertible preferred" share when the shareholder has the possibility of converting his preferred shares into common shares at a given exchange ratio. . . . If the company goes bankrupt, preferred stock holdings are paid off after the bondholders but before the common stockholders.

Preservation of Capital

Term used for a type of investment. Here the investor's primary objective is not the same as in the case of investment for growth or capital gains. His overruling concern is to *preserve* his capital by avoiding high risk situations. He knows there is no totally risk-free investment. He may even use the same vehicles others use, but he will use them with greater caution, staying in for a shorter time or adding other safeguards (such as straddle positions or shorting against the box). He may or may not be especially attracted to preservation via interest income, but he will consider it strongly and use it in part if not exclusively. The image of a capital preservationist used to be someone who sought to hang on to his capital for his old age or for passing on to his heirs. But that image has changed, largely because the risks of loss have increased—mostly because of the international monetary system. It is far easier to lose money today than it was for the last generation. The modern preservationist is not opposed to large profits; indeed he likes them, but he will not put a top priority on them. Investors who have adopted the objective of capital preservation usually approach investments in a totally different fashion from those who are oriented toward capital gains. The latter will always ask before making an investment, "How much can I *make* on that?" The other will ask instead, "How much can I *lose*?" One group of investors is seeking to maximize profit whereas the other group is trying to minimize loss.

Preservation of capital involves far more than just the selection of particular investments. It is even more concerned with the general economic climate, with monetary outlook, with the ebb and flow of recession and boom, than it is with the particular circumstances surrounding a specific type of investment. Thus, especially in recent years, the objectives of capital preservation have become more and more closely identified with an investment strategy that seeks international diversification. It seeks to avoid a too great dependency upon *one* currency and hence upon the ability of the controlling government to maintain the international value of that currency. It advocates holding a good proportion of total assets in reasonably liquid form, for instance in time deposits or government bonds. It calls for diversifying by employing several currencies (especially the hard currencies). It leans toward investments in natural resources—in gold mines, oil, minerals, or an international diversified portfolio of properties.

This type of investment approach is in contrast to the go-go attitude of many investors today who seek to invest in hot new issues or in stocks of companies with a highly developed though often quite unknown degree of technological sophistication or who devote a large percentage of their assets to speculation in commodities and the like. Capital preservation as an investment objective is usually one to which the investor shifts too late, after half or more of his capital has been lost. Usually this objective has been identified with older people. There is a good reason for this: it is quite often only people who have reached a certain age or maturity who have any capital to preserve! But there is an even more fundamental reason: it is usually only people who have experienced the ups and downs of investments over a long span of time who have learned that it is often quite easy to earn money but that it is extremely difficult to keep it. They have seen so many wonder stocks of yesteryear become the failures of today; they have seen so many new, trendy approaches end up in total rejection after the public discovers that there is really nothing new under the investment sun. It would be quite wrong, though, to associate the objective of capital preservation with a negative approach. Investors with this objective will not exclude the shares of major solid so-called growth companies such as an IBM; they will, however, restrict this type of investment to a prudent percentage of their total assets. It seems probable that the objective of capital preservation will grow in importance as the decade of the 1970s progresses, particularly as so many investors in the United States come to the realization that their following the go-go growth investment policies of the 1960s not only did not result in any growth in their personal assets but often produced major and continuing losses.

Price Controls. See **Prices and Incomes Policy**

Price-Earnings Ratio

Multiple at which the price of a stock stands in relation to the earnings per share of that stock. If a company's shares are selling at $100 and the company earns $10 per share per annum after taxes, the price-earnings ratio is 10 to 1. That is, the price stands at a multiple of 10 in relationship to the annual after-tax earnings per share of the stock of that company. Various stocks will show very wide variations in price-earnings ratios. Many cyclical industries (like steel) will have ratios of about 10 to 1. In contrast, the ratio for a company that is supposed to have a tremendous growth potential may stand at 50 to 1 or 60 to 1 or even higher. Among stocks of the computer industry, of electronics companies, and of companies active in areas of advanced technology, such high ratios are common or at least have been. The reason is that investors feel that current earnings are of relatively minor significance in relation to the potential earnings. A stock selling for $100 and earning only $2 per share (thus having a 50 to 1 price-earnings ratio) might still be considered a very good buy if the investor anticipates that earnings will rise to $10 or more per share within the foreseeable future. Such development would allow the company to pay handsome dividends in future years, thus giving the investor a high return. Conversely, a stock earning $10 and selling for $100 might be regarded as a bad investment, even though the price-earnings ratio was "only" 10 to 1. This might be because the company (for example a copper corporation) is reaching the end of the road in ore resources. Exhaustion of their ore reserves means the $10 earnings of today may be reduced to only $2 or $1 five years hence. In such a situation it is possible to find companies selling for a price-earnings ratio of 5 to 1. On average, since the 1960s, shares of major corporations tend to sell at around fifteen times earnings. In bull markets, times of investor euphoria, this average may rise to 18 to 1 or 19 to 1; while in times of recession and investor disappointment the average may fall to 12 or even 10 to 1. In an average market climate, the use of a 15-to-1 price-earnings ratio as a benchmark for judging the ratio of a stock under consideration for investment is reasonable.

The price-earnings ratio is, of course, a tool that is only as good as the underlying statistics. There is no difficulty in determining the price of a stock. But quite often, outside the United States, it is extremely difficult to find out or even estimate the annual earnings of a company. In such countries as France, Italy, or Switzerland or even in Belgium or Holland, the published earnings of a company may grossly understate the true earnings. In light of this, although the price-earnings ratio must be regarded as a prime and indeed an essential tool for investors in the United States, Canada, and United Kingdom, it is often of very limited use in continental Western Europe and in many other areas.

Price-earnings ratios (sometimes simply called P/Es) are applied to the market as a whole as well as to individual shares. In the 1960s it was felt a Dow-Jones Industrial Average P/E of 12 to 1 to 13 to 1 was low (and thus in a buying range), while a P/E of 18 to 1 to 20 to 1 was considered high (and thus a caution or sell signal). The 1970s began with the same psychology, but moods change. In 1949 a P/E of 10 to 1 was thought reasonable for both the market and most shares. . . . An old Wall Street joke used to run (in times of a falling market), "Yields are rallying." These days, with the new popularity of the P/E ratio, one might avoid mention of falling stock prices by saying, "P/E ratios are being revised downward."

Prices and Incomes Policy

British term for programs designed to control prices and wages. In the past, assorted varieties of prices and incomes policies have been tried in many countries, including all the Scandinavian countries, the Netherlands, France, the United Kingdom, and the United States. In all cases the objective is the same; to control inflationary spirals by putting governmental limits on increases in prices and wages allowable in any given period. In every case to date, these attempts to artificially control price and wage increases have failed. What happens in each instance is that, once controls are loosened or eliminated, the market forces that have been artificially pent up explode and the resulting situation is probably no different from what it would have been had no price or incomes policy been implemented in the first instance. Prices and incomes policies have generally been used by socialist governments that do not accept the laissez-faire or semi laissez-faire philosophy of markets and economic managements. They seek to refute the natural laws of supply and demand.

For the private investor, the governmental decision to impose price and incomes policy is generally a bearish signal. What these policies have done, as history shows, is to stifle growth and to therefore negatively affect the confidence of both the business community and the investment community. Conversely, when price and incomes policies are abandoned, in almost every instance there has been a major upswing in business and investment confidence that has led to bullish trends in the securities field. Unfortunately this release from controls is also normally accompanied by inflation of prices, which sometimes more than wipes out the benefits of better business and high numbers on share prices. When this happens (example: the United Kingdom from 1968 to 1972) the inflationary pressures cause the government to return to controls, which again depresses business and investment confidence, and the whole cycle repeats. It's an old story. Controls beget controls, and the precedent of controls makes a return to controls easier, a course of least resistance, however lacking in basic merit.

The most lamentable aspect of prices and incomes policies is that they are attempts to fasten down the lid on a boiling kettle rather than to turn off the fire under the kettle. They are trying to treat symptoms instead of causes. But this of course is the politicians' stock in trade. Once again let me stress an important point for every investor: it is vital in making investment decisions not only to analyze the quality of a bond or the condition and potential of a company whose stock you are thinking of buying; it is equally important to analyze the current situation concerning changes in government policy, especially changes that mean government interference in business and in the financial community. In general one can say that the more such interference there is, the less attractive investments become. One of the keys to investment success is the ability to anticipate changes in the direction of government policy, especially in such strategic areas as prices and incomes.

Primary Trend

In the stock market, a trend in stock values that continues for at least a number of months, usually for several years. Within that primary or major trend, according to classic Dow Theory there come intermediate trends lasting for weeks and minor trends lasting for days.

PRIMARY TREND

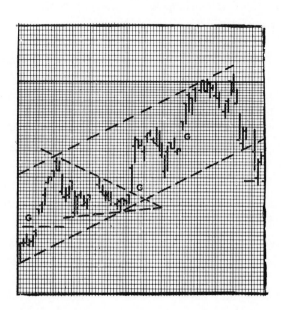

Private Bank

Banking institution that is not organized in corporate form but rather is owned by an individual, a family, or a number of partners. The ultimate backing and security behind the usual bank (a corporation) is its paid-in capital and accumulated reserves—if this capital and these reserves are exhausted, the bank must go into liquidation. In the case of a private bank, the assets—the financial strength and integrity—of the individual owner (or of the owning family or partners) are its ultimate security or capital backing. Private banking was extremely popular in Europe and the United States in the eighteenth and nineteenth centuries. However in recent decades it had become more and more rare. The reason is that, with the growth of banking, it is quite unusual for a single person or a family or a small group of partners to be able to accumulate sufficient capital to match that of the corporate banking institutions. Successful private banks usually at some point go public; that is, the owners change the bank into a corporation and subscribe to a good proportion of the shares themselves but also offer shares to the general public. The bank is then able, with continuing growth, to issue more capital shares to the investing public, keeping the ratio between capital and liabilities appropriate for a bank, normally about 10 to 1. In Europe, in such countries as West Germany, Switzerland, and France, one still finds dozens, even hundreds, of private banks. Normally they do not publish a balance sheet, and therefore it is impossible for a client or customer to have more than a vague idea of the total assets of such banking institutions or of the ultimate family capital backing behind them. It is usual for this type of private banking institution not to concentrate on deposit activities but to act very much like a broker (in the American sense) and to combine this function with the administration of securities portfolios, usually on a discretionary basis.

Private Company

Corporation in which all shares are owned by a private person or group—an individual, a family or group of relatives or bona fide friends, or some other close-knit group of not more than twenty-five people. (See also **Private Bank** and **Public Corporation**.) The Securities and Exchange Commission stipulates that any company with more than twenty-five shareholders must be a public company, and the price of its shares be quoted. Hence, only companies with fewer than twenty-five participants can remain private companies.

Profit-and-Loss Statement

Statement of a corporation showing the income and the expenses during a certain period. If income exceeds expenses, the corporation has operated at a net profit. If the opposite is true, the statement shows the net loss for the period. Profit-and-loss statements usually appear quarterly.

Profit Taking

An investor, after having bought a stock and seen the price go up, sells the security and takes a profit. A bird in the hand is worth several in the bush. He cashes out, taking the profit while he has the opportunity rather than holding in the hope that a still higher price will develop. He avoids the risk of having the price go down and ending up with a loss instead of a realized profit.

Profit taking is of course fundamental to the up and down movement of any stock. It is important for an investor to sense the mood of the general investing public so that he can make the correct sell decisions. It is a basic truth that everyone, whether friend or broker, or banker or investment counselor, is quite prepared to express opinions on what to *buy* and even when to buy it, but it's extremely rare for any such financial people to give advice on when to sell—on when to take a profit. If the stock goes higher, the adviser can be criticized. Besides, most advisers don't have a clue as to when a stock should be sold. Furthermore, selling presents the professional adviser with the problem of having to come up with substitute buys, so it's easier just to let people hold. Inaction is criticized far less than action. Also, people tend to get fond of their shares, and telling them to sell may be like asking them to part with one of their children. Sell advice seldom wins friends; it is highly risky, very difficult to be right about. Yet sell advice is infinitely more important than buy advice. (Telling people when to sell *at a loss* is even harder, for obvious reasons.)

Profit taking can result either from the investor's personal circumstances and feelings or from a general mood that develops in a broad segment of the investing public. It is extremely important that one keep in touch with the mood of the investing public. If one is to take profits it is usually vital to be one of the first in line to do so; for if everyone suddenly decides to take profits at the same time, the inevitable result is a drop, often a very sharp drop, in the level of stock-market prices that can eliminate the profit one wanted to take. *A "safe" rule of thumb is to take profits when they reach 10 or 15 percent.* That is unexciting, but it preserves capital.

The term "profit taking" is likely to be used by financial reporters in describing almost every market dip. But all selling is unfortunately not profitable selling. The phrase looks particularly ridiculous in the press when it is used near market bottoms. It has become a Madison Avenue term that tends to make it appear that people *only* make money in the stock market—they "take profits" when the market falls and obviously make money when it rises. Wall Street, it might seem, just can't lose. But some clients can.

Progressive Taxation

Income taxation under which the rate—the percentage of income which must be paid in taxes—rises in steps as income rises. Progressive taxation began gaining ground only in the 1920s, and the percentages became steeper in the 1950s. Let's suppose a person has an income that for income-tax purposes amounts, after deductions for allowable expenses and the like, to $10,000. On that $10,000 he would have to pay, say, 10 percent in taxes. Let's suppose that for a second person the figure is not $10,000 but $20,000. He, like the first, would pay 10 percent in taxes on $10,000, but on his second $10,000 he would pay a higher rate, say 20 percent. Thus the second man would have a tax bill not twice as high as the first man but rather three times as high. Taking this one step further: a man for whom the figure is $30,000 would pay 10 percent on the first $10,000, 20 percent on the second $10,000, and, say, 30 percent on the third $10,000. His tax bill is $6,000, which is *six* times greater than the first man's. This type of progression in income-tax schedules goes in some countries to as high as 90 percent, but in most countries stops somewhere between 60 and 75 percent.

It is said to be generally accepted that progressive taxation is fair and socially justified; that it is fair for a man who earns a great deal of money to pay a higher percentage in taxes, as measured against his total income, than should a person who is earning at a much lower level, a level that perhaps allows him little more than mere subsistence. Progressive taxation in the final analysis really involves a transfer of wealth from the rich to the poor. Normally all social services provided by the central government or all expenditures made by the central government, be they for medical care or roads or whatever, *help* all citizens to the *same* degree; but as a result of progressive taxation, the individual who makes a lot of money pays more, proportionately, than those who do not. He makes a much larger personal contribution to the financing of these expenditures than the man who has a smaller income, irrespective of the fact that both derive exactly the *same* benefits.

Although it is generally agreed that progressive taxation is an inevitable part of a modern governmental system, there is a great deal of controversy over where the progression should end. It is argued that if the progression continues too far, it destroys one's incentive to earn more, to produce more, to work harder, to contribute to business and thus to the overall growth and prosperity of his country. It is also generally agreed that excessively high rates of taxation in the high income brackets in such countries as Sweden, Norway, the United Kingdom, and increasingly so in the United States, are stifling growth to an unknown degree. For example, extremely successful people in Scandinavia will emigrate to another country and give to it their productive services rather than continue to function under excessive and oppressive taxation at home. It is increasingly conceded that any taxation on income that exceeds 50 percent is self-defeating in terms of national interest. Still, it is doubtful whether nations which today have an excessive progression in their tax structure will move back to more productive levels, since to do so will be extremely unpopular among the less educated voting masses.

Property. See **Real Estate**

Prospectus

Fundamental documentation published by a corporation or a company in connection with the issue of shares or bonds. The idea behind a prospectus is to give a prospective investor the opportunity to thoroughly acquaint himself with the history, financial condition, management, and prospects of the corporation. On the basis of a prospectus it should be possible for a prospective investor to assess possible risks and to make a realistic judgment as to the opportunities and problems which the corporation faces as a result of its current activities.

The art of writing a prospectus has been developed to its highest form in the United States as a direct result of the requirements of the **Securities and Exchange Commission** (see). Every corporation fully subject to the commission is required to reveal in great depth all aspects of its operations. Furthermore, it is stringently required that the corporation shall not in any way exaggerate its potential or the possible future price of the shares (or other types of securities) that it is issuing. The breadth, scope, and rigidity of the SEC requirements have obscured to a large degree the original purpose of the prospectus. In order to protect the issuing corporation and its officers and directors, prospectuses are often no longer written by businessmen but by lawyers who have as their prime object the fulfillment of all SEC regulations rather than informing prospective buyers about the securities in clear language. Also a practice has developed whereby (in its prospectus) the corporation, instead of claiming that anything successful will ever happen in the future, goes to the other extreme, bemoaning extremely heavy competition, expressing suspicions that future profits will be low if not nil, and virtually stating that no one in the corporation really has any belief in its future. Nonetheless, the prospectus is helpful in that it does make full revelations of the financial accounts of the company, revelations that often go much further than those given in the annual reports. Therefore a private investor who desires to go into great depth regarding the financial status of a corporation, perhaps one in which he already owns shares, is often aided by referring to the prospectus issued by that company in connection with the most recent capital increase or bond issue. There he will find much more detailed information on its financial affairs than anywhere else.

In Western Europe as well as in Japan, the requirements are not so stringent regarding the issue or contents of prospectuses in connection with the issue of securities. Often they are two- or three-page affairs that really tell nothing more than the number of shares being issued, their cost, and the banking consortium that will be offering them for sale. Thus it is much more difficult for an investor to get an accurate picture of the condition (especially the financial condition) of a European company than it is on a U.S. company coming under the jurisdiction of the U.S. Securities and Exchange Commission. As a substitute for such data, ask your foreign bank to give you their opinions and data. Swiss banks, for example, have research people who understand the strange European business procedures and know how to "extract" information.

Proxy

Document (a special kind of power of attorney) given by a shareholder of a corporation to another person (usually another shareholder), authorizing the latter to represent him at a shareholders' meeting, that is, to vote for him. It is usual for only an extremely small number of shareholders to turn up for stockholders' annual meetings and exercise their votes directly. It is also usual, where West European or international concerns are involved, for most shareholders to sign over a proxy to the bank that administers their shares. Thus banks often have an extremely important role to play in shareholders' meetings, since they are able to exercise a voting strength that far exceeds their own direct financial interest in the corporation. It is, however, true that such banks, exercising votes by proxy, will almost invariably vote along with the management. In other words, they vote for renewal of the mandate of the existing board of directors. And they almost always vote in favor of any resolution put forward by the board of directors and the administration of a company in its annual meeting. This of course means a good degree of protection for the administration of large corporations: they are practically self-perpetuating because of the great measure of cooperation existing between the institutions holding the proxies for individual shareholders and the administrators of the corporation itself.

Public Corporation (or Company)

Term used to differentiate between a corporation whose ownership is spread among many people (*public* ownership) and a corporation whose shares are held by a very restricted number of people (usually a family), which is termed a **private company** (see). The key differences between a public and a private corporation are whether or not there has been a public issuance of shares and whether these shares are quoted in some type of securities market.

Related to the term "public corporation" is a phrase often heard in financial circles: "going public." By going public, one refers to the process by which the owner of a private company, through an underwriting, makes available for purchase by the public all or part of its shares. This turning point in the history and development of a corporation can be of great interest to the investor. Quite often the shares of a corporation that goes public will rise to a substantial premium over their issue price almost immediately following their initial public quotation. This is often ascribable to the fact that the initial amount of shares offered to the public represents only a small proportion of the founder's stocks. If the corporation is engaged in some new or exotic type of business, if this involves a unique new kind of technology, or if a very well-regarded management stands at the head of the company, the public desire for the stock can cause its price to soar, especially when the number of shares available for public subscription is not great. To be sure, it is the job of the underwriter (the investment-banking concern that manages the placement of the shares among the public) to try to assess the correct price for the public subscription. Nevertheless, often it is the intention of the corporation going public to follow up at later stages with additional new issues to raise money for further development, and both they and their underwriters hope to create a very positive attitude toward the shares on the part of the investment public. Such a positive attitude is of course best created when the original public subscribers enjoy rising prices for the securities they bought.

The chief advantages of a public company are that it gets working capital from the sale of shares without creating debt and that its shareholders have a ready market for their holdings (thus simplifying the passing of their estates to their heirs). However, a public company is subject to much more stringent SEC regulations than a private company. (See also **Going Public**.)

Purchasing Power

What money will buy. Purchasing power is the prime yardstick for judging current and predicting future inflation rates of a country. No matter what rate a government may claim, if the man in the street can buy only half as much with his money this year as last, then the inflation rate for that past year was 100 percent. Purchasing power is a factor to be considered in all investment decisions. When investing, one is not only hoping that the numerical value of the asset will increase (i.e., that its value will go up in pure dollar terms) but also that when one sells the asset, the proceeds will then *buy more* than they would have when the asset was acquired.

Puts

In the United States, options to *sell* a share at a preagreed price. You are selling stock you don't own—thus it is like going short—but with a fixed loss potential as protection. Normally this option is given for 65 or 95 or 190 days. One buys a put for a specific price or cost, in the hope that the share price will go down and that one can then exercise this put (by buying the shares at the preagreed price) and liquidate for a profit, after deducting the cost of the put itself. The opposite of a put is a *call*, the same type of option but an option to *buy*. One of course buys a call option in the hope that the share will go up.

A *straddle* occurs when one ties together a put and a call. A *strap* is the putting together of two calls and one put. A *strip* is the combination of one call and two puts. The average investor does not concern himself with these terms, nor does he understand how puts, calls, straps, strips, and straddles work, for these are techniques which are for the most part restricted to professional traders in New York. *But for those who are willing to do their homework and who seek maximum leverage for their money, the put and call market offers tremendous opportunity.* One can tie up many thousands of dollars of stock for just a few hundred dollars. This element of leverage is both good and bad. It's good in that you make one dollar do the work of ten. It's bad in that you get nothing concrete for your money when you buy an option—it is merely a right to spend your money later. But it is also good in that one's loss is strictly limited. No matter how far the stock moves against you, you can't lose more than the option price, which is usually only a few hundred dollars. Timing is the key with options. (See also **Calls.**)

R and D

Common abbreviation for Research and Development, and usually referring to the funds spent by a corporation for these purposes. Investors should be wary if an item called R and D appears on the asset side of a corporate balance sheet. Often companies capitalize R and D as if it were a tangible asset, in spite of the fact that such expenditure may never result in a viable product and would then have to be written off at a later date, thereby reducing the value of the corporation. (See also **Asset** and **Capitalization**.)

Rand Daily Mail

Well-known South African daily newspaper that gives daily statistics on South African stocks and general news. Address *Rand Daily Mail*, P.O. Box 1138, Johannesburg, South Africa.

Real Estate

American term (unknown elsewhere) meaning land and/or buildings. It's called *property* in the Commonwealth countries, *biens immeubles* in France, *Grundstück* in German-speaking nations. Views differ widely on realty profitability, probably as a result of personal experiences. Many regard the buying of raw land and/or land with buildings on it as the *prime* investment vehicle. In fact, for some people who do think this way, land and buildings on land are often the *only* investments they consider safe. Those who disagree point out that for such an investment one must tie up one's capital, often for long periods. It's nonliquid. When you do decide you want to sell, it can take some time until you find a buyer, even if you price the property within the going price for similar pieces of land. In times of depression it is often nearly impossible to dispose of land and buildings, whereas even at the worst period in a depression, stocks, bonds, and commercial paper do have a market, even if the prices are rock-bottom. Even in boom times a money or credit squeeze can make buyers of real estate disappear. But those in favor of land speculation point out that in times of inflation, real estate becomes highly desirable—fluctuating paper currencies then make it unwise to hold money and difficult to profit from stocks and bonds, for generally those more easily bought and sold do not keep pace with inflation rates. Also, as the world fills up with people and industry keeps growing, unless we learn to build cities in space or on the sea, land *must* have an overall trend upward, even if within that trend there may be temporary setbacks.

However, there *are* areas where real estate may never be worth anything. A piece of the North Dakota prairie, Western Australia desert, or of a dilapidated downtown city area in the eastern United States might never appreciate in value . . . or it might. To buy wisely you have to learn generally about real-estate investment and particularly about the potential of the area into which you buy. A difficult feature of real-estate investment is that no two pieces of property are the same. Every common or ordinary share of General Motors is like every other such share. So are all mint-condition same-date gold coins. So are all AT&T bonds of same date. So are currency future contracts of same date. But every parcel of land, every house, every apartment building, every office rental varies from all others, in location, zoning, condition, age, mortgage, drainage, elevation, climate, and/or distance from schools and shopping, and so on into the night. The variables require a computer to evaluate. These in turn have to be weighed against the economic outlook, monetary tightness or looseness, consumer confidence, etc.

Some people seem to have a "nose" for real estate. But they're rare, and infallibility is unheard of. In summary, to succeed in real estate, you must do your homework. By the way, far more profits have been made in Europe than in the United States in recent decades in property because demand is greater. Land is scarcer and population density is greater. Much of what we say about **objets d'art** (see) is true of real estate, especially as to timing of selling. *It's important to sell well before a boom period hits its peak, because at or after the peak, prices actually obtainable fall fast and customers fade away. Conversely, the time to buy is when no one seems to want it.*

Register of Shares. See **Share Register**

Reserve Currency

Foreign currency held by a national central bank as a means of settling international obligations. The U.S. dollar and the pound sterling are the chief reserve currencies today, and probably account for at least 90 percent of the total stock of world reserve currencies. During the past couple of years the Deutsche mark and the Swiss franc have played an increasingly, though still minor, role as additional reserve currencies.

Residency. See **Domicile and Residency**

Resistance Index

Index to show the amount of movement in the market against what appears to be the primary or secondary trend. If the market is up (as measured by the Dow-Jones Industrial Average), you subtract the number of advances from the number of issues traded. You then divide the answer by the total issues traded. If the market is down, you repeat the process, using the number of declines instead of the number of advances. The calculation can be made weekly or daily. The normal level is between 30 and 60 percent. Any major move in the index shows underlying resistance to the primary trend and means that this major trend should be treated with caution.

Revaluation of Currency

Upward change in the international value of a currency. Under the dollar exchange standard, all currencies of the world are defined in terms of the U.S. dollar. Thus revaluation of a currency means that its value will be greater in terms of the U.S. dollar. An example of a revaluation was provided by the Swiss franc in 1971. Before the revaluation it took 4.30 Swiss francs to buy an American dollar; afterward only 4.08 francs. In other words, the Swiss franc was revalued by approximately 8 percent. In 1971 there were a good number of revaluations, including all of the other major European currencies (German mark, French franc, pound sterling, Dutch guilder, Belgian franc, Italian lira). Additional revaluation took place in 1972 and 1973 in several currencies. The reasons for revaluation are essentially always the same. Certain countries do relatively well in keeping the true rates of inflation in their countries down to fairly low levels. They also keep production high. As a result, their exports of goods and services become increasingly competitive in world markets. This leads to continuing, usually rising surpluses in their trade balances as well as massive balance-of-payments surpluses. By revaluing their currencies, such countries make their exports suddenly more expensive in world markets. In effect they bring their price levels into line with those prevailing in international markets.

Although countries are reluctant to revalue, because they lose some of their competitiveness, they gain by the move. It means their bills abroad (national or private) can be paid off with fewer bank notes than before. It means their citizens get more of everything for less when they travel abroad and exchange their money for others to pay their costs. It means they can buy raw materials at cheaper prices—since their currency is worth more in terms of the seller's currency. They are, in a word, *richer* by the percentage of the revaluation. If you have a bank account in Swiss francs or marks, a revaluation of the currency makes your account worth more overnight; that is, it's worth more when you go to buy another currency, like the U.S. dollar, with the revalued funds. **Devaluation of currency** (see) is the opposite of revaluation.

Rights

In the securities business, one refers to "rights" as the privilege of a shareholder to subscribe to *new* shares being issued by the corporation, in proportion to his prior ownership of shares in that company. For example, often the ownership of two old shares will give a right to subscribe (purchase) one new one. Or, for every three old ones owned, one might get rights to subscribe to two new ones.

Often new shares are issued at a *lower* price than the current market price for the old shares, and a rather complicated calculation is then required to determine what the future value of these shares will be following the increase of capital, since dilution is involved. For example, if for every three old shares, rights were issued for the purchase of two new ones, and if the price of the old shares on the stock exchange is $160 whereas new shares can be bought (subscribed for) under the rights for $140, the resulting future value of all shares, old and new alike (since both old and new will have exactly the same privileges), will be the following: (3×160) plus $(2 \times 140) = 760 \div 5 = \$152$. Such a calculation is important since some shareholders may not want to subscribe to the new shares. In other words, they may choose not to "exercise their rights." In a situation such as the example above, the rights will have a value, in this particular instance approximately $8 per share, which is the difference between the current market value of the old shares and the resulting new value of the stock after the capital increase. These rights can be bought and sold, just like shares.

Safe-Deposit Boxes

Strongboxes in the vaults of many American and foreign banks in which you can store whatever you wish. The boxes can be rented from the bank at a relatively small fee to be paid quarterly or annually. Gold coins, stock certificates, the family jewelry, and valued documents are normally kept in these strongboxes. They probably are most in use in Switzerland, where clients value privacy so greatly. Such boxes in the United States are primarily protection against fire and theft. They are no longer protection against government search and seizure (unless their existence is unknown) via court order. In most countries other than the United States, these boxes are immune from any kind of government intervention. A drawback of bank safe-deposit boxes is that no access is possible during a prolonged bank holiday (as in 1933) or (for a time) in the case of bank failure. Only a few banks provide an outside entrance so that entry and bank closure have no correlation. In a few cities safe-deposit boxes are available in trust companies or department stores that are open during normal shopping hours and have no connection with a bank or banking hours. The demand for such a service is high; the supply is low. Box rental fees have moved up sharply in recent years. The boxes are normally available in several sizes, with rents pegged accordingly.

Scale Orders. See **Buy Orders and Sell Orders**

Securities and Exchange Commission (SEC)

U.S. government agency, the watchdog of Wall Street (and most other streets). It was created in 1934 in the hope that such a disaster as the 1929 crash could be prevented from ever happening again. It watches over all forms of investment, advisers, brokers, floor traders, stock issuance, the stock exchanges, land-purchase schemes, etc., as a sort of Food and Drug Commission for money placement. The SEC has been very useful in requiring that full data be made available to investors. But laws and regulations have never been able to eliminate the opportunities for people to lose money because of such factors as subtle misrepresentation. Morality can't be legislated or enforced. The SEC has simply caused some operators to be dishonest legally. Even so, standardizing the code of behavior in the investment world has, on balance, been of some value. The question always remains, of course, "Who regulates the regulators?" Overall, the SEC is probably regarded by most as a mixed blessing. Its original purpose has not been achieved and cannot be. No one believes it has made another 1929 impossible. It has instead become a police force for all forms of investment.

Sell Orders. See Buy Orders and Sell Orders

Share Capital

Total capital participation in a company; its total direct ownership. Let us suppose that for a corporation in formation it is decided that the basic capital will be $1,000,000. In order to raise this capital, shares are issued. In this case it could well be the corporation would issue 100,000 shares at $10 each. When subscribed and paid for by the shareholders, the money accumulated, namely one million dollars, would be the share capital of the corporation.

Share Register

A volume or volumes in which a corporation records (insofar as formally known to it) the ownership and all subsequent changes in ownership of the shares issued by that company to the public. Required by law of every corporation.

Share(s)

Terms generally used for a document attesting ownership of one or more units of the capital stock of a corporation. Ownership of a share of a corporation means part ownership of that corporation itself in the most direct fashion. The ownership certificates, or shares, are issued by the corporation itself. In the case of large corporations, issuance is often an integral part of what is called an *underwriting*, through which specialty banking houses offer to the public the newly issued shares. Thereafter these documents of ownership can be bought and sold, their price fluctuating according to the judgment of the market as to the overall value of the company. Let us suppose that a company that was originally capitalized at $1,000,000 and issued 100,000 shares at a price of $10 each does extremely well for a couple of years, making excellent profits.

The financial community and the market might judge that the corporation is now worth $5,000,000. This would mean in theory that the price of a share, originally $10, should now be $50.

Short Against the Box

A **short sale** (see). So why the strange expression? Well, the box referred to is a safe-deposit box—yours. If say, near the end of a tax year you feel that a certain stock you own might go down in price and ought to be sold but you know that if you sell it you will be hit with a big capital-gains tax bill you don't want in this year, then you can go short against the box. What you do is to sell short the same number of shares of the stock as you hold "in the box." That way, you make certain of a profit if the price does drop, but you haven't actually sold your shares. At some later date, when you feel able to take the tax bite or you find it advisable for any reason, you simultaneously sell your shares and cover your short sale.

Short Interest

A collective term for the total number of shares that have been sold short on the two major U.S. stock exchanges. These figures are published between the 15th and 20th of each month. Normally the term refers to short sales on New York Stock Exchange short interest, but the American Stock Exchange also publishes short interest figures. A large short interest is deemed bullish, since it is a pool of guaranteed future buyers and they serve to restrain market falls. Conversely a small short interest is considered to be bearish, for there are not many guaranteed buyers and no net under falling prices.

Short-Interest Ratio

A ratio calculated once a month. One divides the NYSE's short interest (the figure published between the 15th and 20th of each month) by the current NYSE average daily volume (volume averaged over one month). When the ratio is about 22 percent or higher, it is bullish, because it means that there are too many shorts for the current volume

and so a lot of them will be forced to cover, causing an upward movement in prices. Generally, below 1 percent tends to be bearish, as it
indicates not much support if prices fall.

Short Sale

If you believe a particular share will fall, you can sell it even though
you don't own it, via your broker, through a stock-borrowing process.
The process is called "selling short" because you are selling what you
are short of. You can buy it later on (you hope) at a cheaper price.
You can sell a stock in New York only if the last previous sale
of that stock has been higher than the one before (an "uptick" as it is
called). This rule was made by the Securities and Exchange Commission
almost as soon as it was created, for it imagined that by not allowing
people to short on a straight down market, it would stop the market
from falling out of the sky. People were so sensitive after the 1929–32
fiasco that any rule that might prevent it from happening again was
welcomed, and this was felt to help the situation. But on the Zurich exchange you can short some U.S. stocks without an uptick. As far as you
the seller are concerned, you are merely placing a bet that the stock
you sold will go lower. In practice, your broker has to borrow the stock
you sell from somebody else—when you "cover the short" you buy the
stock back and he can then return the stock he borrowed for you to
whoever lent it.

There is much rubbish to the effect that short selling is negative, pessimis-
tic, even unpatriotic. It is none of these. It is healthy for the stock market
to have "guaranteed future buyers" (as all short sellers are). It makes
for a more orderly market. Short selling rests on realism, not pessimism,
for no one can afford the luxury of being cynical just for the sake of it
via shorting; the leverage is too costly. And the short seller is no more
unpatriotic than a farmer who sells his grain in a futures market before
he has harvested it. Shorting is simply the result of the investor's opinion
about what is going to happen to a particular share. It is a calculated
business evaluation and decision, as valid as that of the businessman
who sells an asset because he can profit more by leasing it back from
the new owner. The drawback of shorting is that you can lose a lot if
you are wrong. A $40 stock bought long can only drop to zero. But a
$40 stock shorted can go to $100 or $200 or whatever. Bad analysis

here can be very expensive. (See also **Short Against the Box** and **Short Interest.**)

Special Drawing Rights (SDRs)

Created in 1968 by the International Monetary Fund as a means of producing additional international liquidity. They have been given the nickname "paper gold" since their value is defined in terms of gold and, at least theoretically they and gold are interchangeable. In fact, they are merely an artificial international unit of account. (See **International Monetary Fund.**)

Specialist. See New York Stock Exchange

Stagflation

Economic condition in which inflation is increasing with business, on balance, stagnating (some industries up, some down, but overall showing a tendency to mark time rather than move ahead or to actually recede). Apathetic consumer demand is another aspect of the condition. (The term was coined by the author of this book.)

Stock Analyst. See Analyst

Stock Exchange. See Exchange, New York Stock Exchange, American Stock Exchange, Paris Bourse, Swiss Stock Exchanges

Stop Orders. See Buy Orders and Sell Orders

Straddle

Putting together of a call option and a put option. (See **Calls** and **Puts.**)

Strap

Putting together two call options and one put option. (See **Puts.**)

Striking Price. See **Calls**

Strip

Putting together one call option and two put options. (See **Puts.**)

Subordinated Debenture

A type of debenture whose holder has a priority for payment lower than that of other general creditors. Obviously, they are a comparatively risky bond. They sometimes compensate by paying a higher yield.

Surcharge

A charge in excess of the usual or normal amounts; and additional tax, cost, or impost.

SwFr

Abbreviation for Swiss francs. Also shortened to S.Fr. or SF.

Swiss Stock Exchanges

There are three major stock exchanges in Switzerland, at Zurich, Basel, and Geneva, in that order of importance. In Zurich and Basel the German term *Börse* is used for the exchange; in Geneva, the French term *Bourse*.

By far the most important exchange is that in Zurich. It was founded in 1872 and since 1930 has been housed in a special building owned by the government of Zurich and located in the center of that city just one block off the Bahnhofstrasse. The Zurich exchange, like all those of Switzerland, is organized on the ring system. This requires the members of the exchange to stand around a ring and shout their buy and sell orders back and forth to each other. Each business day, trading starts with the security at the top of the list, and trading is conducted exclusively in this security until all buy and sell orders have been satisfied. The members next proceed to the second security on the list, then to the third, and so on. There are two rings, the first being reserved for Swiss securities, the second for bonds and foreign securities. The second ring has developed increasing activity since World War II because many foreign corporations (especially American, German, and Dutch) have listed their securities on the Zurich exchange.

Membership in the Swiss exchanges is restricted to banks. Swiss banks play the roles of broker and dealer and commercial banker, combining all the financial functions under one roof. Their membership on the exchange may be Type A or Type B. Only banks with "A" membership are allowed on the floor of the exchange. These are very restricted in number, there being approximately thirty-five in Zurich and around twenty in Basel and Geneva. The many other banks that have "B" membership must give half the commission to the banks with the "A" membership who do the trading on their behalf on the floor of the exchange.

The Swiss stock exchanges are among the most important in the world, a special reason being that international investors have been attracted to Swiss securities by the high international standing of the Swiss franc. Normally Swiss stocks are priced very high in terms of price-earnings ratios and of yields, because they are often used as currency hedges by international investors who are more interested in having their funds invested in a hard-currency security than in immediate capital gains or yield. It is not unusual to find blue-chip Swiss shares with yields of only 2 percent or less. Another peculiarity of the Swiss stock exchanges is the high prices per share of most of the major issues quoted there. The leading example is the shares of the large Swiss pharmaceutical concern Hoffman La Roche, whose per share price has gone as high as 200,000 Swiss francs, or over $50,000 a share. The average price of Swiss shares is in the range of 1,000 SwFr, or over $250 a share. The Swiss companies don't go much for such gimmicks as stock splits.

There is another peculiarity of the Swiss stock market which warrants attention by foreign investors. Swiss corporations usually issue two types of shares: registered shares and bearer shares. Registered shares require the registration of the owner of the share in the share-registration journal of the corporation. Any transfer of registered shares is subject to the approval of the board of directors of the corporation. Often the voting rights relate to registered shares, not bearer shares. Bearer shares involve no registration whatsoever with the corporation but are simply bearer instruments, like Treasury bills in the United States. It is quite usual for the price of the bearer shares to be substantially higher than that of registered shares. The reason is that Swiss corporations, in order to maintain Swiss control of their corporations, usually will not allow registered shares to be transferred into the hands of non-Swiss. Therefore foreigners who desire to take *equity participations* in major Swiss companies have only the alternative of bearer shares. Thus the price of bearer shares can be at a premium of 25 percent or more over the price of the registered shares. The anonymity of bearer shares may also help increase their price.

An international investor who desires to approach a Swiss *securities market* must first establish a relationship with a Swiss bank, since there are no such things as stockbrokers in Switzerland and the banks have, among other things, a monopoly of the broker function. Normally when one goes to Switzerland for the first time, one establishes a simple bank account with the bank of his choice in Zurich, Geneva, Basel, etc. This account can be used for simple checking purposes or for time deposits in Swiss francs or other currencies; it can also serve as the base for transactions in securities. If you transferred $100,000 to a Swiss bank and instructed it to open an account, your further instructions might very well be to use the funds in the following way: 25 percent to stay as a demand or sight deposit, 25 percent to put into a fiduciary time deposit, and 50 percent to be employed to make purchases on your behalf; it simply credits the securities to your account. It is also possible, and in fact is quite common, for people to buy securities on credit or on margin in Switzerland. The normal margin requirement is approximately 50 percent.

In recent years Swiss-franc bonds have enjoyed growing popularity with international investors, since they represent an ideal hedge for people seeking the safety of the Swiss franc as a hard currency. Bonds, like shares, can be bought only through a Swiss bank. A number of peculiarities in regard to Swiss bonds should be noted. First, by international comparison the interest offered on Swiss franc bonds is very low. In recent years it has been about 6 percent for fifteen- or twenty-year bonds. The reason is again that many foreigners seek refuge for their funds in Swiss-franc instruments, the yield on such bonds being of only secondary importance from their standpoint. Another peculiarity of the Swiss bond market is that it is divided into domestic issues and international issues. This differentiation is made on the basis of whether the corporation issuing the bonds is resident in Switzerland or abroad. In the case of the former (that is, where a Swiss corporation is involved) the interest paid on the bonds is subject to a 30 percent withholding tax. Where international Swiss-franc bond issues are concerned, there is no withholding tax at source. In neither case is there any capital gains tax insofar as nonresidents are concerned.

Switzerland

Financial peace-of-mind haven. Taxes are levied on the income of residents both at the national level and at the provincial or cantonal level. Federal tax is levied at 30 percent and the local tax varies slightly from canton to canton, but is about 10 percent. The one can be offset against the other. Death duties are levied if the deceased was domiciled in Switzerland or left real property in Switzerland. They are based on the value of the estate in and outside Switzerland. Death duties vary from canton to canton, from zero to 4.5 percent if the estate passes to husband, wife, or children; from 2 to 30 percent if it passes to nephews and nieces. Tax liability becomes effective after six months' continuous residence in Switzerland. In the case of foreigners taking up residence in Switzerland not domiciled (see **Domicile and Residency**), taxes can often be negotiated, on the basis of taxation considered fair for the standard of living. That is, if the tax authorities think it costs you $50,000 to live the way you are living, you will be taxed on this amount. Company tax, overall, is about 30 percent per year for companies doing business in Switzerland. On the federal level, holding companies are generally taxed like operating companies; on the cantonal level, however, they are granted some tax concessions. There is a 30 percent withholding tax on interest income from bank accounts. Prices are high, wages the highest in Europe.

Switzerland is not a tax haven in the usual sense of the word. Its taxes are lower than in the United States but considerably higher than *any* accepted tax haven's. Switzerland is a money haven; it has proved over the years to be a safe place to put money, rather than a place where you can put it without tax. This is what makes the current U.S. moves against Switzerland so ironic. There are many tax havens where it is much more profitable to hide money. The man who genuinely wants to stop paying taxes is much more likely to put his money elsewhere than in Switzerland. And he can take his choice of several countries that have relatively good bank secrecy. (See also **Swiss Stock Exchanges.**)

Tape Reading

This can be an art—that of watching the ticker tape as it comes off the machine, which records every transaction, and (because of an inherent good memory) detecting trends in the way stocks are being bought and sold. Tape reading was far more popular several decades ago than it is today, partly because, in the days when market statistics were hard to come by, about the *only* way to follow the market closely was to sit for hours and watch the tape. One must have a feel for the market to be a successful tape reader. Some call tape watching "mental charting."

Taxation

Technically, direct seizure of money or property by the state, backed by the threat of force. It is never optional. There is no free choice. The reason that even in a so-called free society this is accepted is that taxation is always justified on *moral* grounds: in order to live as a community we must jointly provide facilities that we can all enjoy, and we must support the weaker members of our society who cannot do this for themselves. It is the exceptional man who states categorically that all taxation is wrong. However, particularly since the beginning of this century, taxation has ceased to be a method of legislated charity and has become a political weapon whereby politicians tax as high as they can get away with, in order that they can then tell us in their election campaign how much they gave us.

It is a built-in weakness of the democratic system that a politician's first duty is to get reelected, and taxation appears to be his biggest weapon. Many people are gradually realizing that government can only give you what it has first taken away. If people stop demanding more, the government won't be required to provide it, by taxation. The matter requires understanding on the part of both politicians and citizens. Unfortunately, too little leadership is given, too little enlightenment. Many feel that taxes could be cut back to where they were before 1910—under 5 percent—if the government were to get out of the charity, welfare, subsidy, and support business and confine itself to essential services. To achieve this would require a massive educational process and a change in direction, with government no longer to assume the role of father-protector and controller of the economy. The trend in fact seems to be going the other way, toward more socialization or socialism. But tax rebellion is becoming more commonplace, with some citizens refusing to pay their taxes and others leaving their high-tax countries for low-tax havens. (See also **Progressive Taxation**.)

Tax Haven

In its simplest form, a country with low taxes that will allow foreigners to come in, either to reside or more often simply to set up corporate, trust, or other structures to enable them to cut their tax bills at home. In recent years, with the sharp rise in taxation in modern industrial countries, it has become fashionable among small, newly independent nations, or those with very little local wealth, to sell tax-haven status to foreigners in exactly the same way that in the past they used to sell pretty postage stamps and local handicrafts.

Tax havens vary tremendously both in their attitude toward taxation and to the foreigner, and in the facilities they offer. For a fee, all of them will send you a certificate telling you that you are now incorporated and print you a few letterheads—provide you, in sum, with an "instant company." But sometimes this documentation is utterly worthless, assuming you are trying to operate legally, for it does not have adequate substance and meaning. From your tax haven you need good legal facilities, possibly international trading facilities, and a general setup whereby all the people concerned are fully aware that you are setting up a real company or trust and that all the documentation and formalities *must* be adhered to in order to make the entity truly legal. Board meetings, company minutes, profit-and-loss statements, etc., are not required in many tax havens. Once they have sent you your instant company, they are usually interested only in debiting the company account for "directors' fees" once a year, with the "directors" doing nothing whatsoever.

It is frightening to contemplate just how near to being a racket the tax-haven business is in some cases, and just how many unsuspecting people have set up an instant company and assumed very mistakenly that their tax problems were solved. In order to use a tax haven with validity, you must do it on the advice of a tax lawyer in your own country who understands your own tax law and how such companies can be used. You *must* take his advice on how much substance such a company must be given. It is also in your best interests to use a country that takes its own taxation seriously, even if that taxation is low. Setting up a company in a tax haven can also be of great advantage to the international trader, for it gives him a base of operations that is not prejudiced in favor of any single country with which he trades. Also, many havens cater for specific types of international business. Panama, for example, takes great pains to attract the shipping business, and the Shannon Free Zone in Ireland is going to great lengths to attract light industry. Overall, choose your tax haven with care, and do *not* do it alone unless you are very sure of the tax law in your own country.

Tax Shelter

Type of investment that allows the investor to spread his taxable income or capital gains therefrom over a longer period than would be possible in standard types of investment. Examples: oil-drilling consortia and cattle-raising ventures.

Technical Analysis

Term for market analysis that relies on stock charts and statistical indexes.

Term Loan

Bank loan made to an individual or corporation for a specific term such as for two or five years. Generally there is no repayment of principal until the *end* of the term, but it is customary for the interest to be paid to the bank on an annual basis.

Time Deposit

Bank deposit made for an agreed number of days, months, or years at a fixed rate of return. Time deposits yield a higher rate of interest than other deposits because the money is tied up. (See also **Certificate of Deposit** and **Trust Account**.)

Trend Lines

A chartist's term. These are the lines drawn on a chart (usually a stock or index chart) to indicate the channel within which an index or stock tends to move. Although indices and stocks fluctuate considerably on a daily and weekly basis, they have an overall trend that can take

TREND LINES

months or years to form, and trend lines can help the observer detect the general channel within which this trend is forming. Chartists tend to buy stocks when they break out upside from a down channel, and to sell when they break down from an up channel. Every trend is destined to be broken, so trend lines serve as useful guides in plotting one's investment course.

Trust Account (and Trust Agreement)

A trust account of the kind described here is *not* a deposit account in the normal sense of the word, though it *is* a deposit of money. It is an account backed by a fiduciary agreement whereby your bank (very often a Swiss bank) acts on your behalf, by placing your funds with another bank outside the country where your bank is located. Your bank will name the other bank, which will usually be a major institution in London, Paris, Brussels, or Amsterdam. The agreement says that your bank does it in their name, but exclusively at your risk. This means that if the bank in London or Brussels goes broke, the Swiss bank has *no* liability to you. However, since only major banks or branches of very large U.S. banks are eligible for Europlacements by major Swiss banks, the risk in this regard is essentially nil. For their intermediary service the Swiss banks charge about ¼ of 1 percent per annum, a very small fee. Normally the bank will send you the trust agreement for you to sign and return after the actual Eurocurrency placement has been agreed upon (per telephone or telex) and carried out. You need have no qualms about signing. These trust agreements are quite straightforward and have no hookers. Also, while the banks charge a small fee for handling the money, the fact that the transactions go on outside Switzerland means there is no 30 percent Swiss withholding tax to pay on the yield. To set all this in motion, you merely have to make a transfer of funds (or send a check) in dollars (or whatever) to a Swiss bank with instructions. The minimum is normally $25,000.

Underwriting. See **Share(s)**

United Kingdom

Hardly a tax haven. To outline the tax system that applies to British subjects would break your heart. But for an American not self-employed, drawing his income from a foreign source, the United Kingdom can be interesting (not taxwise but civilizationwise). The British tax American residents (and all other foreign residents) on what they call the remittance basis. That is, you are taxed only on money brought into England. If your salary is paid to you abroad, you are taxed only on the amount you bring in. Obivously you have to bring in enough to live on, but you need bring in no more. Britain has a double taxation agreement with the U.S.A. Tax rates for British citizens are among the highest, if not the highest, in the world. Queen Victoria would turn over in her royal grave if she knew what the socialists had done to her free and robust law, tax, and economic legacy. (See also **Double Taxation**.)

Unit Trusts

Term employed in the United Kingdom and most Commonwealth nations for what is known in America as a **mutual fund** (see).

Volume

In market terminology, the number of shares or units of a stock, bond, commodity, etc., that were sold in a given time period, usually one day. It is an American term. In England, the comparable term is *turnover* or *activity*. Precise volume figures are available for the major U.S. and Canadian exchanges, but not for the OTC (Over the Counter) market. Nor are volume figures usually available in foreign markets. Yet volume *makes* markets, so monitoring it is absolutely essential for a high degree of accuracy in forecasting future trends or interpreting present ones.

There are many theories about volume interpretation, some of which seem to conflict, but in fact few do conflict when fully understood. Buying and selling climaxes, for example, are very high-volume moves, occurring precisely at tops or bottoms. But these are relatively rarely seen in market averages (although often seen in individual shares). A somewhat different view holds that when the market appears to change direction and does so on light volume, there is a strong chance the direction change is valid. The reason is that the *quality* of volume is thought to be good at market tops and bottoms. It is only the informed buyer who at the bottom of the bear market will buy "when blood is running in the streets." At the very top the public, in their euphoria, have invested all their cash and run out of buying power, and the market falls for lack of new buying. According to another view, when a trend has been in existence for some time, while volume increases the odds are that the trend will continue for a while.

To chart daily market volume is useful. A ten-day moving average is a favorite to show the trend in volume. Volume is usually at its highest *before* a top or bottom, especially in market averages. A volume theory on individual shares says that it is far more significant if a stock lost, say, three points in a day with a *lot* of people trading it (showing that there were far more sellers than buyers) than if the stock lost ground with very few trading, when it could merely be lack of interest rather than selling pressure that pushed the price down. All accepted line-and-bar chart patterns take note of volume in conjunction with price movement, and indeed a number of market indicators are based entirely on volume.

Wall Street Journal

One of the largest-circulation newspapers in the United States, in spite of the fact that most of its coverage is of financial events. It is the only nationwide daily paper. Most U.S. businessmen feel they must read the *Wall Street Journal* if they are to keep up to date on the financial happenings in New York and if they are to receive depth coverage of the financial status of major U.S. corporations. The *Wall Street Journal* tends to present the facts in its news stories without editorial comment. It is very sketchy and spasmodic in its coverage of any happenings outside the United States.

Wedge

A chart pattern. Wedge formations look a bit like triangles but are more elongated. They are frequently (but not exclusively) seen at minor or intermediate turning points, and thus are especially useful for trading operations. A wedge is a formation where the price gyrates between converging straight lines. In a wedge pattern, both lines slope. A rising wedge indicates a market soon to fall; a falling wedge indicates one about to rise. A rising wedge usually occurs on light volume, whereas a falling wedge starts with quite heavy volume that decreases rapidly as the formation develops. The rationale behind the formation is that the trend comes to an end simply because of lack of investment interest in the move up or down. The volume disappears, and so the stock or market has to reverse, at least temporarily. The wedge is one of the most dependable of all chart patterns. It gives you a price objective, namely to return to the base price where the wedge began. Often the price goes not a step further, but sometimes this is merely the first stage of a major move.

WEDGE FORMATION

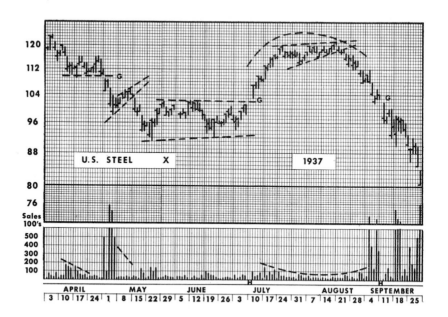

U.S. STEEL X

1937

Week Orders. See **Buy Orders and Sell Orders**

World Bank. See **International Bank for Reconstruction and Development**

73 74 75 76 77 10 9 8 7 6 5 4 3 2 1